# Buddhist Voices in Unitarian Universalism

# BUDDHIST VOICES IN UNITARIAN UNIVERSALISM

Wayne Arnason and Sam Trumbore, Editors

SKINNER HOUSE BOOKS

BOSTON

Printed in the United States

Cover and text design by Suzanne Morgan

print ISBN: 978-1-55896-706-9
eBook ISBN: 978-1-55896-707-6

6 5 4 3 2 1
16 15 14 13

Library of Congress Cataloging-in-Publication Data

Buddhist voices in Unitarian Universalism / Wayne Arnason and Sam Trumbore, editors.
    pages cm
  ISBN 978-1-55896-706-9 (pbk. : alk. paper)—ISBN 978-1-55896-707-6 (ebook)  1. Unitarian Universalist churches—Relations—Buddhism. 2. Buddhism—Relations—Unitarian Universalist churches. 3. Spiritual life—Unitarian Universalist churches. 4. Spiritual life—Buddhism.  I. Arnason, Wayne B. (Wayne Bergthor), 1950- editor of compilation.
  BR128.B8B8345 2013
  289.1'32—dc23
                                          2013002612

We gratefully acknowledge permission to reprint the definitions for some of the Glossary terms which appear on pages 219–234. The definitions for the following terms originally appeared in *Zen Master Who?: A Guide to the People and Stories of Zen* by James Ishmael Ford, published by Wisdom Publications (2006): *Amitabha Buddha, arhat, bodhisattva, Buddha, Ch'an Buddhism, dharma, dukkha, jukai, koan, lay ordination, metta, precepts, rakusu, samadhi, sesshin, shikantaza, soto, sutra, Theravada, vinaya, vipassana,* and *zazen.*

To the founders of and inspiration for the
Unitarian Universalist Buddhist Fellowship:

Robert Senghas, Dorothy Senghas,
Henry Finney, and James Ishmael Ford

# Contents

# FOREWORD

Anyone interested in awakening the inner mind, opening the heart, and co-creating a better world today will be delighted to hear the unified voices in these pages. This highly positive, diverse, and thoughtfully interwoven collection of essays can help us to empower and embrace others and lift them up in their own eyes. It also provides original research and anecdotes about the very first historical intimations of East-West spirituality, as well as the earliest initiatives of Buddhists in America almost two hundred years ago.

I deeply appreciate lineage, traditional erudition, and vital, life-saving debate and discussion. They are the purling streams of any tradition's lifeblood. We find them here in these articles from Buddha-like meditating ministers, as well as an abundance of provocative ideas.

Buddhism and Unitarian Universalism value many of the same things, including experiential practice, study and self-inquiry, mindful awareness cultivation, insightful wisdom development, and loving-kindness, combined with active compassion in the world. This is the heart of sacred activism—empowering, educating, edifying, elevating, transforming, and liberating. Since the mid-1800s, the Unitarian Universalist movement and its two original denominations have helped Buddhism adapt to the New World. They also helped modernize isolated Japan during the Meiji period 150 years ago. The open and eclectic nature of the interface between Unitarian Universalism and Buddhism is almost uniquely situated to contribute meaningfully to our secular, post-denominational, postmodern age.

Not unlike Unitarian Universalism, Buddhism is not so much a religion as a spiritual way of life. It is psychologically and morally astute about character development, ethical values, and the karmic law of cause and effect. It does not require a particular set of beliefs and allows people to explore and discover everything for themselves. Buddhist practice and life depend not on a supreme Creator or on others to liberate or save us, any more than does psychoanalysis or some great world religions such as Taoism and Confucianism. Both traditions follow the Golden Rule—treating others as you would like to be treated—and what I call the Diamond Rule, too: seeing the light, the divine, in everyone and everything, which helps us naturally to actualize and fulfill the Golden Rule. This is a harmonious convergence of East and West, the higher ground within. It is an infinite yet direct journey, from the head to the heart and from me to *we*.

Father Thomas Merton once wrote, "I see no contradiction between Buddhism and Christianity. . . . I intend to become as good a Buddhist as I can " What's the point? Be what you are. Recognize yourself as another Christ. Live so Christ-in-me is "throbbing with life."

Be Buddha now; that's my message too. Not a mere Buddhist, but an authentic, enlightened *Buddha*. In this anthology, Sam Trumbore quotes the nineteenth-century minister James Freeman Clarke, "We speak of going to heaven, as if we could be made happy solely by being put in a happy place. But the true heaven, the only heaven that Jesus knew, is a state of the soul. It is inward goodness. It is Christ found within. It is the love of God in the heart, going out into the life and character." I second that motion, and that emotion.

We are all Buddhas at heart. Our true spiritual task is to awaken to who and what we are, recognize ourselves and each other, and awaken together—for a better world and a better future, which begins now.

Here in one book we have a courageous band of esteemed clerics and wise elders, joined together in their nonsectarian UU-Buddhist sympathies, expounding on their practice and spiritual lives without fear of reproach. To this open-minded and global-visioned initiative, I put my palms together in reverence and awe, with gratitude to these wellsprings of clarity and compassion—and I bow low, with all my heart.

Those with ears to hear, here now know thySelf. Let the love-light in and out, breath by breath, with blessings, attention, and delight.

Lama Surya Das
Concord, Massachusetts
February 2013

# Introduction

This book brings together for the first time the voices of Unitarian Universalists who have become Buddhists without sacrificing their UU identity and Buddhists who have found in Unitarian Universalism a spiritual home where they can sustain a practice and join in an activist religious community that accepts and encourages who they are. This book also looks at the ways that American Buddhism has been influenced by Unitarian Universalism and how UU congregations are being changed by Buddhist practice.

In 1844, Elizabeth Peabody published in *The Dial* the first English translation in the West of the *Lotus Sutra*, one of the most highly regarded Buddhist scriptures. At the time, neither she nor the Unitarian divines who came to her bookstore to discuss Transcendentalism could have imagined the conversation that would ensue between Buddhism and Unitarian Universalism over the next century and a half. The *Lotus Sutra* was one of several "ethnical scriptures" that those who created *The Dial* believed deserving of a respectful reading in Christian America. To use "Buddhist" as a companion identity to "Unitarian" would never have crossed their minds.

In the next hundred years, there was very little contact between UUs and the Asian Buddhist immigrants who founded the Buddhist Churches of America using a Protestant congregational model for their temples. With liberalized immigration laws during the second half of the twentieth century, that allowed Asian teachers of Buddhism to live in North America, the conversation between Buddhism and Unitarian Universalism began to include active Buddhist practitioners. Since 1965, the influence of Buddhist teachings on the spiritual outlook and practices of Unitarian Universalists has steadily grown. While a small minority of UUs identify themselves as both Buddhists and Unitarian Universalists, a much larger number of UUs acknowledge that Buddhist insights have had a significant impact on how they understand and practice their UU faith and understanding.

During the 1960s and 1970s, popular interest in Buddhism among Unitarian Universalists was mostly either academic or exploratory. UUs viewed Buddhism as one of the great world religions that had an important message for UUs, conveyed mostly by simple summaries of Buddhist teachings, snippets of *sutras* (canonical scriptures), and quotes from teachers. UUs began reading books about Buddhism written by Westerners, notably Alan Watts, and visiting retreat centers where they could personally encounter Buddhist teachers. Buddhist practices provided a framework—a language—that could be used to talk about the spiritual meanings of new experiments in consciousness and community that were emerging in Western culture during these decades.

In the early 1980s, UU Buddhist practitioners whose interest had been sparked during the 1960s and 1970s and who had sustained their practices in parallel with their membership in a UU congregation began to communicate and act as a UU Buddhist fellowship, through small gatherings for mutual support and practice. They began to encourage and lead practice opportunities in congregations, usually in the form of groups gathering to share sitting meditation. The growing ranks of Western teachers from various Buddhist schools and the ubiquity of books, retreat centers, and practice opportunities during the 1980s resulted in a larger and stronger UU Buddhist fellowship during the 1990s, with dozens of sitting groups, and with more well-known UU leaders actively identifying as Buddhists.

As ministers offered more sermons inspired or informed by Buddhist teachings, Unitarian Universalists in the pews began to learn more about Buddhism and to engage with the stereotypes that many of our members held about Buddhists. In the 1960s and 1970s, UUs who were suspicious of ritual, authority, and formal religious practices saw Buddhism as doctrinal, hierarchical, and passive around

issues of justice. By the 1980s, more UUs understood Buddhism as a religious tradition that is diverse and varied
in its approach to doctrine and hierarchy, and that it can
be a powerful foundation supporting justice-seeking as a
spiritual practice for individuals and communities. Most
importantly, during the 1980s, Buddhism's nontheistic
orientation began to be more deeply appreciated. Humanist Unitarian Universalists began to recognize that some
devotional Buddhist practices were not tantamount to
worshiping Buddha as a god.

This collection of essays proceeds from the past to the
future, with personal storytelling, personal reflective essays,
and critiques forming the core of the book. The introductory section, "History and Context," has essays by the
editors that introduce Buddhist theology and practice to
those unfamiliar with Buddhist teachings, and that describe
the evolution of the UU Buddhist Fellowship. Jeff Wilson's
essay makes a valuable contribution to UU and Buddhist
history by describing the important role Unitarians played
in hosting the first Buddhist to travel to America and in
exploring the Buddha's teachings.

The "Encounters and Journeys" section contains personal stories of how Buddhist teachings and practices
have made a difference in the lives of leading Unitarian
Universalists. The authors include not only active and
committed practitioners who identify as both Unitarian
Universalists and Buddhists but also UUs who have made
practices taught by Buddhists an important part of their

religious lives. Meg Riley describes how adopting a Buddhist meditative practice that she learned attending retreats has influenced her life. Judith Wright, one of the rare UUs who has a deep Tibetan Buddhist practice, tells us about her spiritual journey as a Unitarian Universalist and practitioner within three Buddhist traditions. Catherine Senghas describes the evolution of her Zen identity and how it influences her urban community ministry. Marni Harmony's homespun essay on creating her symbolic Zen robe, her *rakusu*, invites us to consider how Unitarian Universalism is smiliarly composed of many bits and pieces, all of them meaningful and important. Ren Brumfield tells the story of his journey from the African-American Baptist faith of his birth into a Chinese Pure Land Buddhist community and identity which he found affirmed and respected in a UU church. Alex Holt writes about the desire and delusion of addictive behavior and how his Buddhist practice has moved him toward sanity. The essay by David Dae An Rynick (co-abbot of a Zen temple and a member and former Board chair of a UU congregation) raises important questions about whether and how a dual religious commitment can truly be practiced, and how and when one identity or the other assumes more importance. Joyce Reeves is nostalgic about the UU community that was once part of her life and wonders about whether and how her Buddhist practice has taken her away from it.

The "Reflections" section includes essays from five UU ministers who identify as Buddhists, reflecting on theological themes and issues drawn from their own practice and experience. Kim K. Crawford Harvie offers a very personal narrative of her experience in a vipassana meditation retreat and its application to her life. Wayne Arnason unpacks the Great Vows of Buddhism and their meaning in his life. Sam Trumbore tells us how his practice has made him both a better Unitarian Universalist and a better Buddhist. Doug Kraft suggests strategies of navigating difficult times based in Buddhist understandings and practices. Meredith Garmon takes us on an autobiographical tour of the relationships he has found between philosophy and Buddhism, as someone who has taught both of them.

The final section, "Divergence and Influence" presents reflections from four unique and different voices. Kat Liu's perceptions of how UUs practice Buddhism are informed by growing up in a Buddhist household. Jeff Wilson offers a different kind of contribution here—a reflection on Buddhist, American, and Unitarian Universalist cultures and how they mesh. Thandeka, a UU minister, scholar, and consultant, looks through Buddhist-influenced eyes on the present and future of UU congregations. Finally, James Ishmael Ford, the first UU minister to receive full authorization as a Zen Buddhist teacher, offers a personal reflection on how the Buddhism he teaches and the *sangha* (community) he has created are in an interdependent web of relationship with the Unitarian Universalism he embodies.

A glossary that includes Buddhist theological terms used throughout the book—words often expressed in

Sanskrit, Pali, Chinese, or Japanese—offers further support for readers.

Although identified Buddhists and Buddhist practitioners continue to make up less than 10 percent of the UU population, the Buddhist voices in the denomination are playing a significant role in shaping UU consciousness. We hope that these essays will not only help our readers understand that role but also enhance the dialogue between UU Buddhists and UUs with other faith perspectives.

We are deeply grateful to all our contributors for the gift of their voices, their hearts, and their practice. May all beings be well, and free from suffering.

# HISTORY AND CONTEXT

# Buddhism 101

## Sam Trumbore

Unitarian Universalists discovering Buddhism for the first time will find this primer helpful in introducing basic Buddhist ideas and concepts encountered in the later chapters. There are numerous different schools or "lineages" of Buddhism Each has a wide variety of guiding texts and practices. But, thankfully, all the different Buddhist traditions do share a common story and set of truths, values, and principles that are briefly described below. For further reading, a list of recommended books and a glossary of Buddhist terms can be found at the end of this book.

The Buddha focused like a laser beam on one problem and one problem only, that of human dissatisfaction, suffering, misery, and unhappiness—what he called *dukkha*. On the eternal questions of the nature of divinity, immortality, and ultimate reality, the Buddha remained mostly silent. He recognized that getting answers to these speculative questions one way or another wouldn't address or help people solve the dukkha problem.

Unitarian Universalists are keenly interested in this same problem. Unlike other religious traditions, we are not trying to escape this world and get to another one. We want to learn how to live in this world, experience happiness and peace, and extend that happiness and peace to all beings. The Buddha had a lot to say about all this and also had a way to bring it to life.

Born to a royal family over twenty-five hundred years ago, the young Prince Siddhartha enjoyed fine food, stimulating music, dancing and athletics, and beautiful companions, while being protected from the outside world by the walls of his royal compound. Curiosity about what lay beyond those walls encouraged him to find a charioteer and explore his father's kingdom. Legend has it that on these excursions he encountered people he had never seen inside his walled, protected life. He saw a very sick person along the side of the road. He saw a very old person, too. Then came the shocker—a decomposing body lying next to the road. Finally, he saw a homeless monk who had abandoned his worldly ways to practice a holy life.

These encounters profoundly affected the young man in the prime of his life. Is this, he asked, what awaited him as he aged? Would this be the misery that all the people he loved must face? Was there any solution or was escape possible? The prince vowed to find out.

Siddhartha was hardly the first person to have asked

these questions. Many different scholars, masters, and gurus lived and taught during his time. He studied with the finest teachers and is said to have mastered their teachings and practices easily. He quickly learned that the conditions of existence itself are the source of human suffering. Sickness, old age, and death cannot be avoided. Yet trying to avoid them is our constant preoccupation. And when we have a break from fear, desire steps in and drives us toward things we experience as pleasant, and we seek to hold on to them.

Siddhartha settled on an extreme ascetic practice, seeking to eliminate all sources of desire, resisting all forms of aversion, and hoping to achieve union with what is beyond worldly experience. In the process he practically starved himself to death. Only when the shadow of death came very near did he realize this path of worldly rejection would not solve the problem of human misery. He broke his fast, took nourishment, and sat under the *bodhi* tree—a sacred fig tree with heart-shaped leaves located in Bodhgaya, India—vowing not to arise without an answer.

Amazingly, he got one. He experienced a complete and total cessation of desire, aversion, and ignorance, which solved the dukkha problem. He knew he had the solution, through his own experience of that cessation. It was possible to reach the end of human unhappiness, and there was a way to get there. Siddartha took a new name in recognition of this achievement: Buddha, which means "one who is fully enlightened."

That way he called the eight-fold path, which is really what Buddhism is all about. The Buddha laid out a way of life and a way of mental training and practice that gradually and sometimes suddenly leads people to the direct, personal experience of the cessation of the causes of their unhappiness.

The eight-fold path consists of practicing virtuous moral behavior; cultivating the powers of the mind; and developing wisdom through the experience of insight, directly verifying the reality of the truths the Buddha taught.

Those wishing to follow the path laid out by the Buddha are instructed to begin by practicing virtuous ethical behavior. The Buddha defined five precepts as the foundation for ethical action: refraining from killing, refraining from lying, refraining from stealing, refraining from sexual misconduct, and refraining from clouding the mind with intoxicants. Three of the eight steps on the eight-fold path expand these basic precepts. Right (or skillful or wise) speech consists of speaking the truth in a warm, friendly, and gentle way, saying only what is necessary. Right action is framed by kind and compassionate behavior, honesty, respect for the belongings of others, and harmless sexual activity. Right livelihood requires choosing wholesome, life-affirming occupations that avoid involvement with armaments, slavery, prostitution, slaughtering animals, or selling intoxicants and poisons.

Virtuous behavior, all by itself, can bring much inner peace. In addition to the beneficial effect on one's personal relationships, it helps to calm the mind, making it ready for mental training.

The Buddha taught that human beings have the ability to directly witness the truths of existence. However, since our minds are clouded by greed, hatred, and ignorance, we can't penetrate the mental fog to see them. The first method to clear up some of the clouds is to practice virtuous behavior. The second method, which helps tremendously, is learning to quiet down mental activity through the use of right, or one-pointed, concentration. Developing a concentrated mind requires skillfully directed (or right) effort.

Most religious traditions include methods for reaping the benefits of a concentrated mind. Today many people stumble on these benefits of concentrating the mind by activites such as knitting, running a marathon, becoming engrossed in a novel, or just watching birds on their back porch. The Buddha advised that some capacity to quiet the mind is necessary to hold the attention still enough to observe moment-to-moment experience—what he described as right mindfulness. The method he recommended to develop a calm and clear mind is meditation. Meditation practice uses methods of focusing the mind to calm and quiet mental activity so mindfulness can arise. The mind needs to be quiet enough so that when sensations, feelings, or thoughts arise in the mind, the meditator knows it. And when they pass away from consciousness, the meditator recognizes that they have passed out of consciousness. The illusion of permanence is penetrated through mindfulness.

Wisdom arises from witnessing this process in action. This is the reason for the focus on the present moment. The causal connection between arising sensations, feelings, and thoughts can be directly seen in one's experience as they arise in the present moment. Watching this process and knowing it is happening in the present moment leads to the experience of insight.

The insight or wisdom that arises from directly watching the truths of existence manifesting in one's own experience can be independently verified. The eight-fold path begins and ends with those truths. The four noble truths—the unsatisfying qualities of existence, the maladaptive human response to them that result in our misery, the real possibility for the cessation of that misery, and the path that can lead to that cessation—are the truths to be contemplated on every step of the eight-fold path. The wise intentions that guide each step include resisting desire through letting go; resisting anger and aversion through good will; and resisting violence, cruelty, and aggressiveness through harmlessness.

It is a challenge to practice these intentions, because we are deeply conditioned to impulsively chase desires and to react thoughtlessly with anger and aggression. These are two of the five hindrances that interfere with realizing the cessation of human stress and misery. Weak attention, sleepiness, and boredom dull the mind, making it feel bogged down. Restlessness and worry agitate and scatter mental attention. But of the five hindrances, the hardest to work with is doubt. Doubt manifests itself as a lack of conviction in the value of the eight-fold path and a lack of confidence that cessation of misery is possible.

These hindrances, like all phenomena, can appear to be outside of our control. Thankfully, all of them have antidotes to remove their power to control our minds. Letting go, generosity, and renunciation help with desire. Good will, loving-kindness, and nonviolence help with anger and ill will. Movement, rest, nourishment, contemplating the brevity of life, and applying more effort toward concentrating help with mental dullness. Cultivating calm and rapturous feelings through deepening one's concentration help quiet the restless mind. Remembering the example of the Buddha, reflecting on the many people who have attained enlightenment in the last twenty-five hundred years, the inspiration of the Buddhist teachings, and one's own past success help ameliorate doubt.

In addition, there are seven factors that can be cultivated and that lead toward awakening. Three of them—diligence, curiosity, and joy—bring stimulation and energy; another three—tranquility, concentration, and equanimity—bring stillness and peace. The last—mindfulness—balances the other six.

The end of the eight-fold path, the experience of cessation or *nibanna* (*nirvana* in Sanskrit), both tantalizes and intimidates the seeker of awakening. On the one hand it promises a cure for the chronic mental illness that makes life at times seem unbearable. On the other, it demands the letting go of every dependency, preference, and comfort. The eight-fold path is anything but linear and may take many lifetimes to traverse.

These Buddhist concepts can feel a little alien to Unitarian Universalists shaped by either a Jewish or a Christian worldview that sees time as linear and with an up or down destination at the end of life. The sweep of time in Buddhist thinking is immense, sometimes measured in *kalpas,* almost seventeen-million-year chunks, according to one Buddhist text. But belief in reincarnation is anything but required to find value here. The Buddha was fully human. His accomplishment is possible for every human being. No supernatural intervention is required to make progress on the path. Yet it isn't an easy path for most of us.

One place of connection between Buddhism and the Jewish and Christian tradition is unconditional love. In Buddhism, the cultivation of *metta*, or loving-kindness, is an intentional practice of non-greed and non-hatred. The practice of metta all by itself brings much relief of unhappiness to oneself and others. An immense commitment to love is offered through vowing to become a *bodhisattva*, one who dedicates countless lifetimes of rebirth to work for  the enlightenment of all sentient beings so they are relieved of their suffering.

The best way to get value from the Buddhist tradition and teachings is to refrain from focusing on the end point. The eight-fold path is fruitful in the beginning, fruitful in the middle, and fruitful at the end. Each step along the path can bring greater joy, tranquility, concentration, equanimity, insight, wisdom, compassion, and loving-kindness. Just concentrating on the next step is sufficient to make progress.

—<o>—

**SAM TRUMBORE** *has been a student of Buddhist mindfulness meditation since 1985, studying with teachers who are part of the Insight Meditation Society in Barre, Massachusetts. He is a former president of the UU Buddhist Fellowship and currently serves as secretary. He has served congregations in Niagara Falls, New York, and Port Charlotte, Florida. He currently serves the First UU Society of Albany, New York. He is married to Philomena Moriarty Trumbore and together they have a grown son, Andrew.*

# A BRIEF HISTORY OF UNITARIAN UNIVERSALIST BUDDHISM

## JEFF WILSON

Buddhism and Unitarian Universalism have a long history of encounter and exchange, a history that is little known even to contemporary Buddhist Unitarian Universalists. In 1778, twenty-three-year-old Hannah Addams of Medfield, Massachusetts, began work on an encyclopedia of religion. For the next thirty-nine years the book went through many editions and was quite popular—in fact, Addams was the first American to earn a living solely through her writing. Along the way, her investigations of religion led her to become a Unitarian. Each edition of the book contained more and more information about non-Christian traditions, including significant information about various types of Buddhism in the East. The relative open-mindedness toward learning about other religions which Addams displayed became one of the defining characteristics of the emerging Unitarian denomination. Therefore, it was Unitarians more than any other group that eventually took up Buddhism as a puzzle to be solved and a new source of potential spiritual inspiration in the nineteenth century. For these Unitarians, Buddhism was an exotic foreign faith, one which alternately shocked and—as a philosophy detached from practice—tantalized them. It broadened their ideas of what a religion could be and led them to reflect on the attributes of their own religious tradition.

At the same time that Unitarians were slowly coming to understand that such a thing as Buddhism existed out there beyond the Pacific Ocean, events were taking place in Asia which would soon have an impact in the heart of Unitarian America. In 1841, five Japanese set out from home to fish. Like most Japanese of their day, they were steeped in the Buddhist tradition, mainly Pure Land Buddhism, one of the most popular traditions of Buddhism in East Asia, with elements of the Shinto nature religion. While they were fishing, the sky turned black and a storm arose. The waves tossed their boat back and forth until their oars were smashed and they were driven far out to sea. For thirteen days they drifted on the sea, until they came to a tiny island where they were stranded for months.

But then one day, while the youngest of the five— fourteen-year-old Nakahama Manjiro—was scouring the beach for food, he saw a gigantic ship approaching. The men on board were like nothing Manjiro had ever imagined: Some had red hair and blue eyes, while others had dark skin and curly hair. The strange sailors proved to be friendly and took them aboard.

The ship was a whaling vessel out of New Bedford, Massachusetts. Its captain, William Whitmer, had the men fed and clothed. He suspected they were from the forbidden country of Japan, and if so, he would not be able to return them to their home. Japan had officially been closed to the outside world after Catholic missionaries in the seventeenth century brought turmoil to the country. Thereafter, foreigners who landed in Japan were put to death. In fact, the castaways had already broken the law by leaving Japan, even though accidentally, and to return home now would be a capital offense. Thus, Captain Whitmer kept them aboard as he turned the ship back east and headed for the Kingdom of Hawaii.

During the long voyage, the young Manjiro made a strong impression on the captain. When the ship reached Hawaii, the four Japanese adults were let off, but Manjiro decided to travel to the United States. Upon reaching New Bedford in 1843, Manjiro, now known by his adopted English name, John Mung, became the very first Japanese person to ever visit the United States.

In New Bedford he encountered a new religious landscape, dominated by Protestant Christianity. Manjiro began to learn this new religion, but he faced obstacles. His English was improving, but Whitmer's Methodist church refused to allow the nonwhite Manjiro to join in their services. So Manjiro and the captain joined the Unitarian church across the river in Fairhaven instead, a congregation filled with religious liberals and abolitionists. Manjiro became perhaps the first nonwhite Unitarian, and he readily soaked up the new ideas he was exposed to. Under the influence of the Unitarians he became an individualist, a proponent of racial equality, an advocate of modern science and education, and a believer in God and the Bible. He nevertheless retained aspects of his childhood Buddhism as well, making him, in 1843, the first Unitarian Buddhist. In New Bedford he studied English, mathematics, and navigation, becoming exposed to a world of knowledge unknown in his native land.

Meanwhile, the New England culture Manjiro was struggling to understand was becoming increasingly interested in foreign cultures and religions. Just as one Unitarian woman, Hannah Addams, had inaugurated American learning on Buddhism, so a second Unitarian woman produced a milestone in American Buddhist history. In 1844 Unitarian Elizabeth Peabody's partial translation of the *Lotus Sutra* appeared in the Transcendentalist journal *The Dial*. Under the guidance of Henry David Thoreau at the time, *The Dial* was one of the foremost journals of liberal religion. Peabody's excerpt was the first English translation of a Buddhist *sutra* (canonical scripture). Appropriately, she chose a section of the sutra that describes how the rain of the *dharma* falls on all plants equally, and they take it up according to their needs and abilities. Thoreau himself was much enamored of the Buddhist writings that he encountered, declaring in *A Week on the Concord and Merrimack Rivers* that "I know that some will have hard thoughts of me, when they hear their Christ named beside my Buddha, yet I am sure that I am willing they should love their Christ more than my Buddha, for the love is the main thing."

In 1849 Manjiro decided to try his luck in the gold rush out West. It proved to be a dream come true, and he quickly made a fortune. His transformation from impoverished Japanese fisherboy to wealthy American self-made man now complete, he booked passage to Honolulu, and from there was able to get himself and the three surviving members of his original band of castaways passage on a ship due to sail near to Japan. Even though the ship could not dock in Japan, Manjiro had a plan to get the party home, and he gambled that the knowledge they brought back would be valuable enough for the authorities to spare them punishment. Manjiro bought a small boat and had it stored aboard the ship, and when they finally came within sight of Japan, he lowered his craft into the water and the four men paddled to shore. The year was 1851, and Manjiro had finally come full circle.

However, his ordeal was not over yet. He and his companions arrived in Western clothing with strange accents acquired overseas. Officials were immediately suspicious of them, wondering if they were foreign spies or, worse yet, Christians, or both. Anyone who sojourned among the barbarians on the other side of the sea was a lawbreaker and a potential threat. The officials decided that the men must undergo *e-fumi*, the ancient test for weeding out Christians, that went back to the time when Roman Catholic missionaries had destabilized the country. Suspects were told to stomp on a picture of the Virgin Mary and her child. The Japanese knew from their experience with Catholics that Christians would refuse to step on a holy icon and therefore would forfeit their lives. But the Japanese didn't know about Unitarians, who as radical Protestants had no special devotion to Mary and did not view icons as holy. Manjiro casually stepped on the image, passing the test.

Accepted now in his homeland, Manjiro immediately became an important person in Japan. He had been trained in Western sciences, mathematics, and naval techniques and had encountered hundreds of technological inventions undreamed of by the Japanese. His importance grew even more two years later in 1853, when Commodore Perry's American flotilla (sent by U.S. president and Unitarian Millard Fillmore) arrived, forcing Japan to open to the West. The *Shogun* (military dictators) summoned Manjiro to help them deal with the new threat. Manjiro became an official advisor and rose to the rank of samurai. He advised the government on American culture, taught English, translated foreign books, and composed the country's first textbooks on English. He also exposed his countrymen to the ideals of democracy, individualism, social equality, and liberal Christianity. A group of young turks gathered around him. These included Sakamoto Ryoma, a major architect of the coup that established the modernist Meiji regime, and the father of Japanese democracy. They also included Manjiro's closest partner in the drive to modernize Japan, Fukuzawa

Yukichi. A tireless reformer and promoter of education, he founded Keio University and was instrumental in bringing Western learning into Japan.

In 1868 came the greatest upheaval in Japanese history, when the Shogun was overthrown by the rebellion fomented by Sakamoto Ryoma and his comrades, installing Emperor Meiji as ruler. An aggressive modernist, Meiji opened Japan wide to trade, knowledge, and missionaries from the West. Life changed for every Japanese. This new opening of Japan also brought ever more information about Japanese religion to America. Many curious Unitarians eagerly lapped up this new knowledge. A significant part of the intelligentsia of the age, Unitarians became disproportionately exposed to Buddhism, and spread ideas about the faith widely. Through family bonds, school ties, shared publications, and pulpit exchanges, they developed a remarkable network of liberal religionists that not only knit together America's spiritual and intellectual cutting edge, but stretched across the oceans to other parts of the world.

An example of this network is the case of Fannie Channing, grandniece of the Unitarian founding father William Ellery Channing. She married Englishman Sir Edwin Arnold in 1864, inducing him to sometimes attend Unitarian services, and he eventually took up Unitarian views of Jesus without renouncing his Anglican membership. In 1879, fifteen years after his marriage, Arnold published *The Light of Asia,* the most important nineteenth-century work on Buddhism in English. A highly appreciative book-length poem on the life and teaching of the Buddha, *The Light of Asia* was a major bestseller that went through numerous editions.

Some common features can be found in the writings on Buddhism by Unitarians of the second half of the nineteenth century. The authors approached their subject with Protestant assumptions. The most obvious example was their claim that the oldest kind of Buddhism—the kind closest to that of the historical Buddha—was the only authentic Buddhist expression. Further evolutions in Buddhism were seen as degenerations. Their near universal respect for the Buddha as a man mirrored their Unitarian admiration for Jesus as a moral and rational teacher. They referred to the Buddha as a sort of Asian Jesus: pure, chaste, self-abnegating, kind, pacific.

Universalists also began learning about other religions. Perhaps no Universalist of the age contributed more to exposing his fellow Americans to other cultures and religions than the king of showmen, P. T. Barnum. Barnum was greatly interested in foreign cultures, and his museum included numerous Buddhist artifacts from overseas. Even greater, however, was his obsession with elephants, and it is here that Barnum contributed significantly to American Buddhism. In 1884 Barnum heard that the king of Thailand had a sacred white elephant. Enchanted by the idea of a white-colored elephant worshipped by Buddhists, he arranged to buy the pachyderm and have it shipped to New York. But when the beast climbed down from the ship, Barnum found he'd been hoodwinked. The elephant wasn't snowy white as he'd imagined, but an albino with pinkish, patchy skin. Having spent considerable money and advertised his coming attraction far and wide, there was nothing Barnum could do but take it on the road with his circus. In order to make it a better show, however, Barnum imported a second shipment from Thailand—a group of Thai monks to walk around the ring with the elephant and chant in Pali. Thus, as a result being hornswoggled during his attempt to humbug, P. T. Barnum brought the very first Theravada Buddhist monks to America.

The Universalists were influential in other ways as well. For instance, Universalism experienced a major brain drain in the mid-nineteenth century, when many ministers defected for the ranks of Spiritualism—a new movement that sought spiritual answers in the emerging nexus of proto-psychology, religious naturalism, spirit beliefs, and liberal Christianity. In their communications with the paranormal realm, these Universalists and former Universalists often received messages not only from Jesus, angels, and famous Christian figures but also from Hindu, Buddhist, and Chinese spirits.

For example, one of the most influential Spiritualists, James M. Peebles, resigned from the Universalist ministry in 1856 due to stress and ill health. This freed him to travel. While in California in 1861, he met a Chinese immigrant named Le Can, whose religious insights impressed Peebles so much that he felt ashamed of how Americans had boasted of their superior religion and civilization. Peebles wrote about how he began to be visited by Asian spirits, who conveyed ancient secrets of Oriental wisdom. He studied non-Christian religions along with Christianity and Spiritualism, convinced that the spirits would have revealed religious truths to people in all cultures and traditions. He traveled extensively in Buddhist countries and eventually proclaimed, "Briefly put, I am a Christian, a Spiritualist, a Buddhist, a Freethinker." From their place within Spiritualism, the Universalist Spiritualists were an early vanguard of post-Christian liberals who propagated the value of all religions—particularly Buddhism—to their denominational Universalist friends, as well as to members of other denominations who were interested in the widely popular Spiritualist fad.

Meanwhile, in Meiji, Japan, Fukuzawa Yukichi, Manjiro's greatest disciple, worked tirelessly to modernize Japanese society. Fukuzawa had learned about Unitarianism from Manjiro, and Fukuzawa intended to bring this rational religion to Japan. He petitioned the American Unitarian Association to send missionaries to his country. In 1887, Rev. Arthur Knapp responded to his call. Knapp's Unitarian mission was not based on the same sort of Christian triumphalism that characterized other American projects in Japan. As quoted in *The Unitarian Movement in Japan*, he told Fukuzawa,

> The errand of Unitarianism to Japan is based upon the now familiar idea of "Sympathy of Religions." With the conviction that we are messengers of

distinctive and valuable truths which have not here been emphasized, and that in return there is much in your faith and life which to our harm we have not emphasized—receive us not as theological propagandists, but as messengers of the new gospel of human brotherhood in the religious life of mankind.

Knapp was soon joined by other important American and British Unitarian missionaries. And three American Unitarian professors arrived not long thereafter. They were put to work by Fukuzawa, teaching in his Keio University, the most modern educational institution in the country. It was designed with the liberal and scientific ideas Fukuzawa had learned from the Manjiro. Fukuzawa declared himself a Unitarian, as did many others. A Unitarian meeting hall was built, and a popular Unitarian journal was founded.

Unitarianism attracted many Buddhists interested in reforming Japanese Buddhism along Unitarian lines. Knapp, in an article in 1890, discussed the relationship between Buddhism and Unitarianism as he saw it. He identified five points of similarity. First, in contrast to traditional belief in creation as a historical fact, both Unitarianism and Buddhism conceived of creation as a continuous process without beginning or end. Second, in contrast to orthodox Christian belief that the soul was something given to humans at birth, Unitarianism and Buddhism regarded the spirit as something eternal and divine in its nature. Third, both Unitarianism and Buddhism were based on the principle of *karma*, which concerns the effect of our actions on our paths to enlightenment. Fourth, while both Unitarianism and Buddhism honored their founders, neither regarded them as absolute or as deities. Fifth, neither Buddhism nor Unitarianism was based on old traditions or tales but on human reason and natural principles.

Unitarianism made significant contributions to Meiji Buddhist thought, with practical consequences for how Buddhism was practiced, propagated, and represented to the West as well. Some of the most important Buddhist reformers of the time period became Unitarians. These Buddhist Unitarians actually called for a union of Buddhism and Unitarianism into a new religion of the future. They rejected as superstitious the Christian elements of Unitarianism, and understood Unitarianism instead as a set of principles. They sought to use Unitarianism to rework Japanese Buddhism as a rational, scientific, liberal religion. The treatment of Unitarianism as a set of principles by the Japanese instead of a supernatural belief system mirrored much of the American Unitarian thinking about Buddhism, which considered Buddhism in terms of high-minded philosophy but rejected the seemingly superstitious elements of Buddhism as practiced by Asian Buddhists. Buddhist Unitarian organizations, such as the Bukkyo Seito Doshikai (translated as Association of Buddhist Puritans), were founded, and they published their own journals, such as *Shin Bukkyo* (meaning New Buddhism).

The Unitarian-derived modernist principles helped Japanese Buddhists turn the tide of the anti-Buddhist movement infecting state-Shinto-dominated Meiji Japan. But ultimately the anticipated union of Buddhism and Unitarianism did not come about. This was primarily because the Unitarian missionaries refused to abandon their commitment to an explicitly Christian understanding of Unitarianism. As this became clear to the Buddhist Unitarians, the Unitarian mission began to peter out in the second decade of the twentieth century. However, this Unitarianized Buddhism continued to develop on its own trajectory within Japan. Most of the Unitarian Buddhists belonged to the Jodo Shinshu school of Pure Land Buddhism, the most widely practiced branch of Buddhism in Japan. The Unitarian Buddhist reformers used their Unitarian training to further modernize Pure Land Buddhism.

A second, smaller stream of Buddhists in Japanese Unitarianism were Zen adherents. Zen Buddhism emphasizes personal enlightenment and direct insight through meditation rather than scripture and doctrine. Some of Zen Buddhists also directly used Unitarian principles to reform Zen, but even more interesting are those who adopted Unitarian principles without making an explicit connection to Unitarianism. Perhaps the most important of these was Shaku Soen, a major Zen reformer of the Meiji era who imbibed Unitarian-influenced religious thought as a student at Fukuzawa's Keio University. Another Zen practitioner who also attended Keio and was influenced by Unitarian thinking was Shaku Soen's famous disciple D. T. Suzuki. Together, these two men were largely responsible for introducing Zen to the West over the next sixty years. The process began at the World's Parliament of Religions in Chicago in 1893 (partially organized and strongly attended by Unitarians and Universalists), where Shaku Soen read a speech translated by Suzuki.

The Zen Buddhism which Shaku Soen and D. T. Suzuki presented to the West was already partially Unitarianized in Japan before it ever reached America. This was due to the influence of Fukukawa Yukichi and his Unitarian professors at Keio, but also because Suzuki admired Ralph Waldo Emerson as one of the most important spiritual leaders of modern times. Soen and Suzuki sought to remake Zen into an intellectual, scientific religion that was less about faith and more of a set of natural principles—precisely the way the Japanese had understood Unitarianism.

By the turn of the twentieth century, a new figure emerged to export Unitarianized Buddhism to America. Yemyo Imamura was deeply influenced by Fukuzawa while studying at Keio University. Imbibing the modernist Buddhism of Fukuzawa's circle, Imamura became determined to adapt Jodo Shinshu Pure Land Buddhism to the spirit of the times. As bishop of the Buddhist Mission of Hawaii (beginning in 1900), Imamura worked to establish a partially Unitarianized Jodo Shinshu among the immigrant Japanese community there. His role in the plantation labor strike of 1920 made him America's first major socially engaged Buddhist. He also ordained the first Euro-American Pure Land ministers and fostered ties with the non-Buddhist community.

In the post-World War II period, Buddhism and Unitarianism began to interact on an institutional level to a much greater degree than ever before. Especially important was the role that Unitarians and Universalists played in helping the Japanese Americans being released from American internment camps. In 1945 the First Unitarian Church of Cleveland allowed a congregation of Japanese-American Buddhists to be formed within its church, an act of hospitality repeated in 1946 by the First Unitarian Church of Chicago and in 1965 by the First Universalist Church of Minneapolis. John Haynes Holmes invited a Buddhist Churches of America minister to speak at the the church Holmes served as minister, Community Church of New York (Unitarian), marking the first sermon by a Buddhist to an American Christian congregation. The Japanese-American Pure Land Buddhists were not the only group that received assistance: In 1966 the first Theravada Buddhist temple in the United States, the Washington Buddhist Vihara, was established—it held its meetings at the All Souls Unitarian Church in Washington DC, until temple members purchased a building the following year. This pattern was repeated countless times, and today Buddhist groups meet in well over a hundred UU churches as renters or official church-sponsored groups across North America.

Throughout the twentieth century, Japanese Unitarian minister Imaoka Shin'ichiro, a convert from Jodo Shinshu and the founder of the Japan Free Religious Association, kept alive the Unitarian church in Japan while seeking fellowship with Buddhist denominations. In 1968 he brought together Dana Greeley, president of the UUA, and Nikkyo Niwano, founder of Rissho Kosei-Kai—a new Buddhist movement based on the *Lotus Sutra*—telling the two men they would find much in common. Greeley and Niwano formed a close friendship; Niwano credited Greeley with inspiring him to turn Rissho Kosei-Kai into an activist sect focused on social progress, while Greeley got the idea for small group ministry from Rissho Kosei-Kai. The following year, Rissho Kosei-Kai's six million members joined the newly re-named International Association for Religious Freedom, started in 1900 by Unitarian Charles Wendte. The UUA was the primary player in the Association at the time, and together the UUA and Rissho Kosei-Kai would go on to co-found the World Conference on Religion and Peace, an important international interfaith organization.

Individual Unitarians, Universalists, and Unitarian Universalists also revived the earlier interest in Buddhism. These included Kenneth Patton, the leader of a new brand of Universalism in the 1940s and 1950s that sought to make the Universalist appreciation for world religions explicit. Patton brought Buddhist symbols and liturgy into his church in Boston, and when he was hired to help create the first Unitarian Universalist hymnal, he brought significant numbers of Buddhist hymns into UU practice. Another important figure was Rev. George Marshall, for twenty-five years the minister of the Church of the Larger Fellowship, who published a biography of the Buddha in 1978.

Meanwhile the partially Unitarianized Buddhism already brought to America continued to make its mark on the country's religious landscape. Kanmo Imamura, son of bishop Yemyo Imamura, continued his father's drive toward Pure Land Buddhist reform, Americanization, development of educational venues, and liberal approaches to religion and social issues. His projects included the Berkeley Buddhist Study Group. This liberal congregation was the most important Buddhist institution of the 1950s, providing a venue in which the first Tibetan lama taught Buddhism in the United States. The Study Group also influenced Gary Snyder, Allen Ginsberg, Jack Kerouac, Alan Watts, Taitetsu Unno, Philip Whalen, Robert Jackson, Alex Wayman, and other major figures in later twentieth-century American Buddhism.

Starting in the 1980s, Buddhism began to make major inroads into Unitarian Universalism as a living system to be practiced, not just a philosophy to be studied or a foreign group to associate with. As Unitarian Universalism experienced an identity crisis and moved toward a post-Christian self-understanding, members began to look to other religious traditions for new perspectives, spiritual practices and ethics. Neo-Paganism, Judaism, and Hinduism all played a part in this exploration of new possibilities, but arguably none of them rivaled the eventual ascendance of Buddhism as a source of new ideas.

Some Unitarian ministers became jointly ordained as Buddhist priests, such as James Ishmael Ford. Gene Reeves, former dean of Meadville Lombard Theological School, began writing a column in Rissho Kosei-Kai's English-language magazine *Dharma World*. Other UU ministers also began regularly appearing in the pages of *Dharma World* and speaking to large Rissho Kosei-Kai audiences in Japan. In addition, Rissho Kosei-Kai representatives—sometimes including current president Nichiko Niwano and future president Kosho Niwano—began attending the annual UU General Assembly, where the group has held Buddhist services and workshops for UUs. Perhaps more significantly, a series of eight joint Unitarian Universalist/Rissho Kosei-Kai conferences were held in the 1980s (four in Chicago, four in Japan). Meanwhile, Rissho Kosei-Kai began sending many of its most prominent young students to study at Meadville Lombard.

UUA presidents now regularly meet with Buddhist leaders, including the Dalai Lama, and Buddhist Unitarian Universalists serve on the UUA Board of Trustees. Many UU ministers claim a Buddhist identity or influence. Many more UU laypeople claim an affiliation with or affinity for Buddhism. Children are taught about Buddhism in a sympathetic fashion by the religious education curricula put out by the UUA. Articles on Buddhism appear in *UU World*, the magazine of the UUA. Books promoting Buddhism are published by the UUA-owned Beacon Press and Skinner House Books, and the UUA bookstore offers numerous Buddhist titles—they've even sold a do-it-yourself Buddhist rosary kit.

Over a 234-year span that covers almost the entirety of the nation's history, Buddhism has moved from being an exotic foreign faith of passing interest to American religious liberals to a living religion taken up by many members of liberal congregations. In the process, Buddhism in Asia was partially reshaped by the encounter with American Unitarianism, accelerating the rise of modern Asian Buddhism. Today Buddhist ideas and practices are common within Unitarian Universalism, and the relationship between these two traditions grows ever stronger.

―◦―

**JEFF WILSON** *is an associate professor of religious studies and East Asian studies at Renison University College, at the University of Waterloo in Ontario. He is also an ordained minister in the Jodo Shinshu Hongwanji-ha tradition of Shin Buddhism. He attends Grand River Unitarian Congregation with his family in Kitchener, Ontario.*

# A Brief History of
# the UU Buddhist Fellowship

## Wayne Arnason and Sam Trumbore

The history of the Unitarian Universalist Buddhist Fellowship is a story about people who need each other. People who need each other to support their dual theological identities and to remind one another that this duality is, at the deepest level, an illusion. If living and dying are the focus of both the UU and the Buddhist traditions, we should be more concerned with the unity than the duality between these traditions.

The individualism of Unitarian Universalists who practice Buddhism is often challenged in the Buddhist *sanghas* (communities) in which they participate. And yet, the Unitarian Universalist Buddhist Fellowship (UUBF) has been more individualistic than institutional. It has been primarily interested in supporting personal practice rather than evangelizing others to Buddhism or Unitarian Universalism. While persistent in its survival, the UUBF has expanded only modestly. The organization has stuck to a limited agenda of roles and tasks and has largely done those well, believing that the reach of this sangha should not exceed its grasp. In the stories of its individual leaders, in its program offerings, and in the relationships it has cultivated with American Buddhist leaders, the UUBF is a unique reflection of the history and evolution of American Buddhism.

The UUBF began with individual practitioners—two UU ministers and one layperson. Without the efforts of Robert Senghas, James Ishmael Ford, and Henry Finney, there would be no Unitarian Universalist Buddhist Fellowship.

Robert Senghas came to formal Soto Zen Buddhist practice in 1983, when he visited Zen Mountain Monastery, in Mount Tremper, New York, in its early years of formation under the leadership of John Daido Loori. Senghas was minister of the First Unitarian Church in Burlington, Vermont. In partnership with Henry Finney, a sociology professor at the University of Vermont and lay member of the Burlington church, Senghas began offering a meditation practice group, or sitting group, at the church. As he received the Buddhist moral and ethical teachings (the "precepts"), thus publicly affirming his Buddhist identity, Senghas sought to bring together other Buddhist practitioners within Unitarian Universalism for conversation and support. The Unitarian Universalist Buddhist Fellowship was thus founded in 1984, when Senghas and Finney began compiling a mailing list—the first step toward making a more vital network possible.

In the late 1980s, informal sitting groups convened by UU Buddhist practitioners—both lay leaders and ministers —were gathered out of the local interests and needs of people who wanted to meditate together. These groups were inspired by or connected to a variety of Buddhist schools and teaching lineages that were taking root in the United States and Canada. The Community of Mindfulness founded by Vietnamese Zen teacher Thich Nhat Hahn, several other Zen lineages, and some Southeast Asian schools known as *vipassana* were represented among the early sitting groups in UU congregations. Henry Weimhoff in Brooklyn and Marni Harmony, a minister in Orlando, Florida, were among the earliest sitting-group founders. During this period, Buddhist sitting groups in UU churches were rarely in touch with each other to compare notes or share practice.

The first occasion for those wishing to form a Unitarian Universalist Buddhist Fellowship to gather face-to-face came at the 1985 UUA General Assembly in Atlanta. George Marshall, senior minister of the Church of the Larger Fellowship, delivered a talk on his book *Buddha: A Biography,* published by the UUA's Beacon Press in 1978. Although Beacon had also published Thich Nhat Hahn's first book, *The Miracle of Mindfulness,* there was little published by Unitarian Universalist authors about any aspect of Buddhism. Marshall's speech provided an occasion for Unitarian Universalists interested in or already practicing Buddhism to become aware that a Unitarian Universalist

Buddhist Fellowship was forming. Senghas was the first president. Ralph Galen was the secretary, responsible for the mailing list and communication. Dorrie Senghas, Robert's wife, by now a Buddhist student as well, also served in the initial organizing group.

Initially, the UUBF consisted of only a mailing list. In the days before email, written communications announced events at General Assembly and provided an opportunity for networking among people who had already started or wanted to start sitting groups. Senghas offered a workshop on meditation at the 1986 General Assembly at the University of Rochester, the first presence of a UUBF event at a General Assembly and an important occasion for attracting interest and new leaders.

The group of new leaders included a Buddhist priest, ordained in a Soto Zen lineage, who had found Unitarian Universalism while searching for a spiritual community that could offer family ministry, and religious education for children, which was missing in Zen communities. James Ishmael Ford found Unitarian Universalism to be the only Western tradition where his Buddhist identity was warmly welcomed and where he could pursue a career as a religious leader within both traditions. While completing his Master of Divinity from Pacific School of Religion, Ford met other UUs who were Buddhists or who were discovering Buddhism for the first time. He was ordained as a Unitarian Universalist minister in 1991. During his first settlement in Mequon, Wisconsin, Ford started a sitting group and became interested in expanding the work of the UU Buddhist Fellowship.

In March 1996, Senghas and Ford offered a weekend workshop at Zen Mountain Monastery expressly for Unitarian Universalists—those already practicing Buddhism and those interested in knowing more. That year, Ford published and posted on a UUBF website an essay called "An Invitation to Western Buddhists," a reflection on the natural affinities and possibilities for mutual enrichment between Buddhists and Unitarian Universalists.

The first leadership team of the UUBF was organized by Senghas and Ford in the 1990s. When ministers Sam Trumbore and Wayne Arnason joined them in 1997, the team worked to give the organization more structure by adding Board members who reflected the diversity of Buddhist lineages represented within Unitarian Universalist Buddhist practice groups. Each initial Board member has served as president and helped shape the UUBF's vision and direction.

The UUBF's activities fall into four general areas: publications, electronic communications, UUA General Assembly activities, and odd-year convocations. The earliest and most regular activity has been the publication since 1994 of *UU Sangha,* a newsletter that comes out one to four times a year, depending on the dedication of the editor at the time. Ford was the first editor. Ford persuaded Trumbore to take over the editorship in 1997; Trumbore redesigned and reformatted *UU Sangha*, and the editors who followed—Jeff Wilson, Gerald Bennett, and Robert Ertman—have each innovated and further improved the newsletter. Over the years it has documented the history of people and traditions and the evolution of practice within the UU Buddhist community. *UU Sangha* has given voice to Unitarian Universalists, particularly ministers, as they have explored connections between Unitarian Universalism and Buddhism.

Early on, *UU Sangha* began publishing a list of Unitarian Universalist Buddhist practice groups. The list increasingly filled the back pages of the printed publication as more and more groups asked to be listed. In 2006 the UUBF began posting that list on its website.

The UUBF had established a basic website in the middle 1990s to archive back copies of *UU Sangha* and to provide some introductory information about Buddhism and Unitarian Universalism. The group launched its first email discussion list around the same time. Before the arrival of Facebook, Twitter, and cell phone texting, this list was an important tool for connecting UUs exploring Buddhism. Many fruitful conversations grew out of these email exchanges. Sometimes the list would become quiet and someone would post a question asking if the list was alive. Someone would respond that the stillness of the list is exactly what you might expect from people who meditated.

Beginning in 1998 the UUBF Board of Trustees decided to build connections among Unitarian Universalists interested in Buddhism at General Assembly. At the time, workshop slots at GA were not hard to get. The Board reserved a 75-minute slot for a public presentation and another slot for an annual meeting. Starting in 1999 the Board invited Buddhist teachers and scholars sympathetic to Unitarian Universalism to present at GA. Sandy Boucher, Doug Phillips, Lama Surya Das, Tara Brach, John Tarrant, Ruben Habito, Barbara Kohn, Melissa Myozen Blacker, and David Dae An Rynick all participated in these workshops. A presentation by Buddhist scholar Rita Gross on women in Buddhism concluded this series in 2007. After 2007, these appearances by Buddhist teachers before national UU audiences ended when General Assembly was restructured to limit the number of workshops available to independent but related organizations outside the UUA. However, the presence of UUBF at General Assembly has been maintained by a booth in the exhibit hall, and in 2012 the UUBF offered a well-received worship service, featuring a guided meditation led by Arvid Straube.

The biggest project taken on by the UUBF has been to organize weekend convocations, inspired by the successful practice of the UU Christian Fellowship. The first UUBF convocation took place in the spring of 2005 at the Garrison Institute, a retreat and events center in Garrison, New York. It began on a Thursday evening and ended Sunday at lunch, and drew about 130 people to hear Jeff Wilson, Zen Roshi John Daido Loori, Tibetan Lama John Makransky, and MBSR (Mindfulness-Based Stress Reduction) teacher Beth Roth each give presentations. Between presentations, the participants were assigned to small groups to discuss what they were learning and to explore the connections between Buddhism and Unitarian Universalism. Inspirational opening worship by the Board and closing worship by Kim K. Crawford Harvie framed the retreat. This first convocation powerfully shaped the growth and development of the UUBF.

The second convocation, in 2007, again met at The Garrison Institute. This time Roshi Bernie Glassman and Eve Myonen Marko were the theme presenters. The Faithful Fools Street Ministry from San Francisco also came, to help participants explore the connection between Buddhism and social justice work.

The 2009 convocation took place at the historic Mission San Luis Rey in Oceanside, California, organized in part by Board member and minister Arvid Straube. This convocation centered around the teaching of Shinzen Young, a student and practitioner in several Buddhist traditions. This event was more practice oriented and educational than the three previous convocations. It attracted fewer attendees but served as a catalyst for supporting West Coast UUBF practice groups.

In 2011, the UUBF convocation returned to the Garrison Institute. This time James Ishmael Ford and David Dae An Rynick, founding teachers of the Boundless Way Zen, were the guest teachers. Ford and Rynick worked together on several traditional *koans* (teaching stories or verses), introducing participants to non-traditional communal koan study. The UUBF held its 2013 convocation at the Pearlstone Retreat Center near Baltimore, featuring Tara Brach as guest teacher. The Fellowship intends to continue to use the convocation as a major biennial gathering of UU Buddhists.

In each *UU Sangha* publication, presentation at GA, and convocation, the interaction among participants has been just as important as the information presented from the authors and speakers. The most stimulating and transformational work of the UUBF happens in the question-and-answer periods, in the hallways, and over the dinner tables. The UUBF is at its best when it serves as the vehicle to connect Unitarian Universalists to Buddhism and Buddhists to Unitarian Universalism. When the two meet, learning, growth, and development spontaneously arise. In that creative interchange, the UUBF fulfills its mission.

# ENCOUNTERS AND JOURNEYS

# STANDING ON THE
# SIDE OF METTA

## MEG RILEY

In the 1980s, as a young adult, I was terrified that the world was going to end imminently. The buildup of nuclear arms permeated my days and brought me nightmares. Wanting to do something, I joined with a small group of peers to begin street theater actions around nuclear weapons.

Some of us had done street theater before, related to violence against women, and had found it empowering to speak up loudly and visibly until we got kicked out of the grocery store, laundromat, or office building where we performed. Instead of helping us feel more empowered, however, the street theater we created around the nuclear arms race made us more feel even more scared and hopeless.

I don't remember which one of us brought Joanna Macy's book *Despair and Personal Power in the Nuclear Age* to a meeting of our empowerment group, but it became our Bible for the next four years. We left the streets and instead rotated to each others' houses, and an occasional retreat center, to work the exercises Macy laid out. With the aplomb typical of young adults, we immediately began offering the exercises to others. We didn't care that Macy had adapted ancient Buddhist practice or that she was introducing us obliquely to Buddhist teachings around interbeing—which she defined as "dependent co-arising" and "taking refuge"—we just cared that these exercises allowed us to feel some hope and to sleep at night without having nightmares of a nuclear holocaust.

Admittedly, Macy's book drew from other sources besides Buddhism, as do all her books that carry this work forward—most recently, with Chris Johnstone, *Active Hope: How to Face the Mess We're in without Going Crazy*. So it never occurred to me, from using her work, that there might be more strength and comfort to be found by delving deeper into Buddhist practices.

Fast forward ten years. The woman I was in a relationship with devoutly practiced *vipassana* (insight) meditation, a practice brought to this country by American students of Southeast Asian Buddhist teachers. Moreover, she attended long retreats several times a year and kept hounding me to join her. I was too busy, I kept saying—busy as an activist in Washington DC, busy running around trying to save the world in the name of Unitarian Universalism. For years, she sat on the cushion for me. I can say that because I know I drew peace and strength from her practice through noticing how it changed her. I noticed that when she returned from retreats she had a deep glow that lasted for weeks. I noticed that when I was hyperventilating in an anxiety attack about the latest atrocity I faced she could breathe deeply and smile.

Finally, after eight years of her asking me to do so, I agreed to join her in a weeklong retreat. Keep in mind that I hadn't sat in meditation for fifteen minutes since the 1980s, so this was a fairly weird thing I'd agreed to do. I agreed because it made her so happy, and I felt safe in the conviction that I would actually *not* be able to go. We were in the throes of adopting a child, and I was sure that we would be in China when the retreat came up. When it became clear that we would not be in China after all and that my whining was not going to cause her to say, "Oh you poor thing, don't come if you don't want to!" the fear really set in. A week without talking? Without reading? What if I died? Actually the fears took very concrete shapes, and I found myself following her around like a small child with frightened questions. "Has anyone ever thrown up on the *zafu* (meditation cushion)?" "Has anyone ever peed in their pants?" I don't know what I pictured, but clearly I was scared.

*Vipassana* meditation is more gentle than Zen, and this was good for me. I had sat in the Zen meditation style known as *zazen* during college for a flicker of a moment, and I did not find that to be a positive experience. All attention seemed to be on a form which I could not master, and then I sat in a stream of self-hatred about that. This vipassana retreat, led by American Buddhist teacher Tara Brach, was a kinder and gentler experience. I found that the meditation bell would ring to begin and then, seemingly seconds later, the fifty-minute sitting period was over.

In the small group where we processed how the retreat was going, I mentioned this rather happily. I had feared I would be bored silly, yet here I was, whipping through the sitting sessions without a shred of pain or discomfort! When Brach heard this, however, she did not seem so happy. "You're going into trance," she said. "That's not what we're aiming for here." She suggested I spend the next few days sipping tea and looking at the sky, noting what I saw there among the clouds and birds.

So my first retreat was a quasi-meditation retreat, and I enjoyed it immensely. When it was over, re-entering the world of conversation and interaction felt overwhelming and exhausting. Six months later, when my partner asked me to go on another retreat, I agreed again, even more sure this time that we would be in China, but less terrified when we still were not. At this second retreat I fell in love with sitting practice. That was in 1996, and I've been a fan ever since, particularly of the practice known as *metta*, a meditation on loving-kindness for all beings.

I don't practice every day or anything close to it. But what I like about Buddhism is that it is a practice—for me, it is nothing like the noun *faith*, which I sometimes want to own like a possession, like a rock. Buddhism is a river. As the years have gone by and I have listened to hundreds of sermons, known as *dharma* talks, from teachers, and read more theory, I have found that Buddhist concepts, more than any others, offer me comfort in my most despondent times. Sitting by my mother's deathbed, it's not that I sat there "as a Buddhist." It's that Buddhist language, metaphor, and understanding offered itself to me like a cozy blanket, reassuring me that it didn't matter that my mother called herself an atheist; the life that she lived was still holy. Sitting with the fact of impermanence before, during, and after her death was easy and beautiful. I was neither grasping nor despondent.

The metta practice has been the most specifically useful Buddhist practice that I use, and I use it more often than any other. I do metta in all kinds of situations: reading the paper, sitting in meetings, exercising on the elliptical machine, working in the garden. Metta is a practice of shining the intention of loving-kindness on the world—starting small and gradually moving out to all beings, beginning with myself: *May I be free from danger. May I have ease of well-being. May I be physically happy.* I often offer myself metta when I am in physical or emotional pain.

As an activist, I must be willing to open myself to pain— to understand that, as Lily Tomlin says, "We all time-share the same atoms." I must be willing to connect myself to larger forces and understand that I am part of them. This is hard when I want to distance myself from the perpetrators and align myself only with what is good, or innocent, in the world. Metta allows me to find a resting place in it all. *May all beings have ease of well-being. May all beings be physically happy. May all beings be free from danger.*

In those years in DC, I could feel myself walking the edge of despair and terror. The paths we traveled as a nation felt so wrong; it pained me to stay open and connected. Metta in some sense saved my life, and I began practicing it the way a drowning man stays on his back: For him, turning over means death. I gasped up at the sky, thrown around by waves, with only my tiny words and intention to keep myself breathing. *May we have ease of well-being. May all beings be happy.*

—◁◦▷—

**MEG RILEY** *serves as senior minister of the Church of the Larger Fellowship, a UU congregation without walls. She has ministered in the intersection of faith and public life in a variety of capacities within Unitarian Universalism and the interfaith world. She lives in Minneapolis with her family.*

# "You're a UU Tibetan Buddhist?"

## Judith E. Wright

I am frequently asked about my connections with Unitarian Universalism and Tibetan Buddhism. Often a Unitarian Universalist wonders why I integrate into my life such an esoteric religious tradition as Tibetan Buddhism with my religious path as a Unitarian Universalist. A Buddhist or UU Buddhist may ask me why I have decided to follow a *vajrayana* (Tibetan Buddhist) path. Frequently not only people new to Unitarian Universalism but also Buddhists whom I encounter on my spiritual journey question ask how I can be both a Unitarian Universalist and a (Tibetan) Buddhist. I'll try to answer these questions by sharing my spiritual journey in this life time.

Most UUs are familiar with mindfulness, or insight, meditation, and a large number of UU Buddhists practice in the Zen tradition, but few Unitarian Universalists follow a Tibetan Buddhist path. My interest in Tibetan Buddhism began long ago when I was working as a child psychologist in a rural community mental health care center. I read an article by a Tibetan master and I became absorbed in his description of the dying process. I wanted to learn more. I thought about how different this way of thinking about death was compared to how we normally think about death in the West. Little did I know at that time that this would become a major focus of my spiritual path.

I was already a Unitarian Universalist at the time. I joined the faith over fifty years ago, after I met the Tucker family. They were Unitarian Universalists, living in Columbia, Missouri, who invited my husband and me to dinner to meet their interracial family of three adopted children. Of course, at the time, I had no idea what it meant to be a Unitarian Universalist. I had never heard of the denomination. My husband and I, like the Tuckers, were thinking about adopting children. Eventually we gave birth to two children and adopted two others, all within five years. Ours indeed is a multiracial, multicultural family because we made these early decisions.

Seeking a religious home for our four children prior to the civil rights movement, we remembered the Tuckers and decided on Unitarian Universalism. I became very active as a lay leader in religious education and worship, and spiritually I thought of myself as an agnostic, believing primarily in the material reality that I could see, touch, or measure.

But, as the Buddha taught, all is impermanent. In my mid-thirties, I had a midlife spiritual crisis. I began to question Unitarian Universalism and my own personal spiritual beliefs. Something was missing. I felt a yearning and longing for something beyond a totally scientific, rational approach to religion. Science had been my God for much of my life, and I came to question the limits of a solely scientific worldview. Over time, I came to temper my reliance on scientific thinking with personal experiences that have not yet been proven by science.

Ralph Waldo Emerson's words about "life passed through the fire of thought," in his *Divinity School Address* of 1838, especially helped me see not only the value of experience and the value of reason but also the importance of following my own inner spiritual truths. I began to confront the religious authorities of my congregation, who were mainly humanists and academics in our university town.

My spiritual life was turned upside down in ways that did not fit into any of my previous understandings about reality. Out of left field, I had a number of what I now believe were profound mystical experiences—moments of grace and glimpses of what I now call the holy and the interconnectedness of all. These experiences would lead eventually to my call to the Unitarian Universalist ministry.

Initially I was confused by these profound events. I sought out spiritual teachers—Catholic and Episcopal priests, Quakers, Hindu and Buddhist teachers, and of course, UU ministers—to help me understand what was happening. I found my first connection with Buddhism at that time through The Insight Meditation Society in Barre,

Massachusetts. I sat in meditation with Ruth Denison, Larry Rosenberg, Jack Kornfield, and other wonderful teachers who first taught me how to meditate. For the first time in my life I was exposed to the Buddha's teachings, and they spoke to my heart and spirit. The teachers assured me that I could remain a Unitarian Universalist and still practice Buddhist meditation. I did so. And when I returned to my UU congregation as a lay leader, my minister, David Phreaner, assured me as well that I could follow a Buddhist path and remain a Unitarian Universalist.

During this time, I also read (as a good UU!) everything I could get my hands on about mystical experiences, including, of course, Evelyn Underhill's classic *Mysticism*. When I went before the Ministerial Fellowship Committee to become a UU minister, I described a dream I had of crossing a bridge. I was laden with books—lots of books—and on the other side of the bridge, a warm light invited me. One of my spiritual teachers, Elisabeth Kübler-Ross, stood near the other side, encouraging me to cross over. I was headed into the unknown, into my ministry, and my life as a minister would, indeed, pass through the fire of thought, yet at the same time remain open to ever exploring the unknown. For me, there was and is always mystery. I have come to accept that much in life happens on levels I don't comprehend. My experiences in Buddhism have reinforced this sense of mystery.

Continuing my spiritual search, during long Buddhist meditation retreats I experienced periods of luminosity and light that scared me. During meditation periods of profound light I would ask myself, "Is this the living Christ? Is this the Buddha? What is this light?" and "What would Emerson say about this light? Channing?" Today I lean toward believing that these experiences are examples of what the Buddha taught. Every sentient being has luminosity and clarity of mind. However, I do not, as a good UU, have a final answer about the exact nature of these experiences.

All I can say is that they motivated me, and continue to motivate me to turn my life around—to turn from being a fairly self-absorbed, driven person toward becoming someone who attempts to help other beings and believe truly in the oneness of God, or in the interdependent web of existence of which we are each a part.

During the years I explored *vipassana* teachings, or insight meditation—which aims at helping practitioners gain insights into the impermanence and unsatisfactoriness of ordinary existence—I found that with my undisciplined mind I could easily avoid practicing outside of retreat settings. So I sought a more disciplined approach to meditation.

For the next nine years I became a serious Zen student of John Daido Loori at Zen Mountain Monastery in Mount Tremper, New York. From Daido I learned how to truly sit *zazen*—seated meditation aimed at developing deep concentration and calmness of mind and body, leading to insight into the nature of existence. Daido taught me how to "sit like a rock," and through his powerful presence, his teachings, and my hard work, I experienced profound deepenings of understanding of Buddhism. I became a serious, disciplined meditator.

My approach to Buddhism shifted dramatically in 1999 when I received an invitation to attend the (Tibetan) *Kalachakra* teaching on world peace given by His Holiness the Dalai Lama in Bloomington, Indiana. The *Kalachakra* is one of thousands of *tantras*, or teachings given by the historical Buddha. The Dalai Lamas are particularly fond of imparting this fairly rare teaching. At the center of each tantra is a deity that is regarded as an aspect of Buddha mind. Such deities are not perceived as gods but as personified states of mind that the practitioner strives to attain as he or she journeys toward enlightenment. The Kalachakra practice aims to develop wisdom and compassion within those who receive the initiation and then continue to practice its teachings daily.

I felt compelled to attend this Kalachakra initiation. I had no idea why. After the ten-day initiation, I knew that I had to switch from Zen to Tibetan Buddhism. While I highly value my nine years under Daido's guidance as a Zen student, I had been struggling for some time with feelings that arose within me during my times at his monastery.

A particular incident began to shift me away from Zen Mountain Monastery. One day I was late for the first morning sitting. I had arrived at the monastery late the night before and I thought I had about half an hour before the session began. I arrived at the entrance to the main meditation hall drinking coffee and trying to wake up, unaware of a time change—of which I had not been told—for the morning session. I was not allowed to enter the hall—I was suddenly scolded by a nun, who accompanied me to a sitting area just outside the entrance to the hall, where, confused and somewhat upset, I sat watching what occurred there. I was amazed to observe the teacher enter the meditation hall, followed by his attendants. As he walked around the room greeting his followers and students in a loving way, encouraging each to continue to meditate, the room was filled with luminosity, and my heart was filled with love for my teacher.

I felt a strange mixture of awe and shame that day. It took me a long time to recover from being excluded from that morning's sitting. Years later, when Daido was one of the main presenters at our UU Buddhist Convocation, he spoke of how his approach to Buddhism was a tough one. I agreed with him—this is why I had left his monastery.

When, at the Kalachakra initiation His Holiness the Dalai Lama spoke of "My friends, the Chinese," I was in awe that a leader could maintain such equanimity after the killing of one million of his people. I wanted to learn how to gain such equanimity. He said that the core of a person is gentleness, which contrasted sharply with my experiences in the Zen tradition. As a woman, as a person with a soft voice, as a fairly gentle soul, I had struggled for much of my adult life with even how to survive within the hierarchical, competitive American culture. When I heard His Holiness teach that the core of a human being is gentleness, I knew that I had found my Buddhist home.

I have been blessed with a number of teachings and initiations by Tibetan Buddhist teachers since this initial teaching by His Holiness. I practice chanting, visualizations, and certain *mudras* (hand gestures), and I perform *tonglen* (a prayer-like meditation practice). I have a special shrine room in my home where I meditate twice a day. Each of the initiations and practices that I follow is about a certain deity that represents a quality of mind to be developed. For example, Medicine Buddha is for healing; White Tara for developing peace; Manjushri for developing intellectual powers; and Green Tara for overcoming obstacles.

Over the last ten years or so I feel I have integrated these two strands of religious life: Tibetan Buddhism and Unitarian Universalism. Impermanence, end-of-life issues, generosity, kindness, compassion, and wisdom are just a few of the themes that I blend into both my UU world and my Buddhist practices. I have established and led meditation groups within four different UU congregations. Today I lead two different meditation groups each week in First Parish Northborough, Massachusetts.

In 2008 I spent five months of my sabbatical at Kopan Monastery near Kathmandu, Nepal, a monastery guided by Lama Zopa Rinpoche, who has compassionately allowed Western students to come to Kopan. For the first three months I did a practice named after the *Vajrasattva*, along with fifteen other Western students. This practice is an act of purification believed to help the practitioner let go of negative actions in this lifetime and previous lifetimes. Here I reviewed my life and my many mistakes and regrets and determined to try hard to not repeat such actions. Most of this retreat was silent, and I took the eight vows of Mayahana, the larger of the two major traditions of contemporary Buddhism. I spent the last two months in Nepal at the the Khachoe Ghakyi Ling Nunnery, where I was blessed to teach nuns advanced English and enter into their daily lives. My experiences at Kopan led me to accept reincarnation as one of my central religious beliefs.

As my spiritual life continues to unfold, I am drawn to Tibetan Buddhist practices related to the passages at the time of death. As a UU minister and as a Buddhist practitioner, I hope to help and comfort others at the time of death. I am also preparing myself for this most significant passage, when I too will drop this body and move onto what is next.*

I have been blessed to receive teachings on *phowa* from Ayang Rinpoche, phowa master from Nepal and India. Ever since I read about the Tibetan Buddhist approach to dying years ago, I wanted to learn how to do phowa—a yogic and meditative practice of the transfer of consciousness at the time of death. It is believed that when a person dies,

---

* See Judith E. Wright, "End of Life Passages and Tibetan Buddhism," *Unitarian Universalist Psi Symposium Annual Journal*, 2011–2012, pp. 4–16.

his or her consciousness can be ejected by a person who has learned phowa from a master. I hope to be able to eject my consciousness at the time of my death. No one should attempt to do phowa without initiation and permission from a qualified Tibetan Buddhist master, such as Ayang Rinpoche.

When asked how I can be both a Unitarian Universalist and a Buddhist, I can easily respond that both traditions have blessed my life and transformed me. Isn't that what makes religion worthwhile? Unitarian Universalism provided a safe haven for my four children as they grew up in a racially intolerant world, and it infused me and all in my family with principles to help us lead happier lives. It has led me to remain open and curious about whatever arises, and to use a balance of reason and intuitive experiences as touchstones along my spiritual journey. My UU connection has provided me with external pathways of great meaning: beloved community, spiritual companionship, core values, and justice-seeking work.

The Buddhist part of my search has led me internally toward a deeper understanding of a science of mind. Buddhism, like Unitarian Universalism, encourages me to question and doubt and not to take on teachers or teachings without testing the merits of each. Indeed, I take heart that His Holiness the Dalai Lama states that if science proves a particular Buddhist belief incorrect, he will side with science. Buddhism has shown me a spiritual path that I deepen through meditation. In addition, Buddhism has given me a framework to work with my inner life, transforming it into healthier ways of being through letting go of negative mind states such as fear, attachment, desire, and anger. Buddhism has also given me avenues to open my heart and spirit to positive states of mind, such as loving-kindness, compassion, and the interconnectedness of all. It has also given me a belief in life beyond this lifetime, and so much more.

Both Unitarian Universalism and Buddhism have provided me with spiritual companions, fellow travelers as we search together for the truths of our lives. We live within a context of mystery. We are part of a larger whole that we can sometimes, if we are fortunate, understand. Both traditions call us to value and celebrate life and yet not become too comfortable with what is—choosing instead to cherish ourselves and all life and to make the world a better place for all. These are just some of the many reasons I have remained a Unitarian Universalist Tibetan Buddhist.

—◦—

**JUDITH E. WRIGHT** *is in her eleventh year as the settled minister at The First Parish Church, Unitarian Universalist, in Northborough, Massachusetts. She has previously served congregations in New Jersey and Rhode Island, and hospitals in Philadelphia as a chaplain. She regularly attends teachings at Namgyal Monastery in Ithaca, New York, the Dalai Lama's monastery in North America. Judith has four grown children and six grandchildren.*

# FULLY ALIVE

## CATHERINE SENGHAS

Three weeks after my cherished aunt died, I darkened the door of a Zen teacher she had told me I should go see. My aunt had been a Zen practitioner for well over a decade, and I watched as she lived the last year of her life with pancreatic cancer with a magnificent grace that her Buddhist way made possible. As she was dying, she was fully alive. I wanted to know more about how she was able to do it

I was a midlife seminarian when I went to that Zen teacher. I had already left the Catholic tradition in which I was raised and had become a Unitarian Universalist. I found it hard to explain why I abandoned the faith into which I was born and raised. I just knew it wasn't the right religion for me, ever since I was a young adult.

During my spiritual transition, I carried with me a deep appreciation for my birth faith's formative influence on my life. The caring mentors, the rites of passage, the ages-old sense of community rooted in shared values all carried over into my new ideal of religious community.

From the perspective of seminary and midlife, I could look back and recognize that I left because of ecclesiology —the structure and doctrines of religion—and theology —the foundational understanding of nature. Unitarian Universalist ecclesiology suited me well when I joined this faith tradition in my early thirties, and our fourth Principle's covenant to affirm and promote a free and responsible search for truth and meaning opened me up to a lifelong quest. Now that quest was taking another turn.

Although I found Buddhist theology and history some- what interesting and informative, I felt drawn primarily to the practice. Just sitting. *Shikantaza.* I discovered that I was not able to engage in sitting meditation in the traditional Zen posture—full lotus. Luckily, that ability is not a prereq- uisite for meditation in the extended *sangha* (community) I found. As I continued to sit shikantaza, the practice began to open up my manner of experiencing each moment, my manner of being awake. In the same way that practicing yoga had attuned me to awareness of my breath, shikantaza has attuned me to the activity of my mind.

For some years, along with my solo practice, I sat faith- fully every week with a sangha. My current situation doesn't permit that regularity, but on Monday nights I sit virtually with them by meditating at the same time they are gathered. I am deeply committed to at least one annual five-day *sesshin* (an extended meditation retreat) with our larger sangha.

Today, with seminary and my own decade of Zen practice behind me, I've had to wrestle with and make more explicit what it means for me to identify as a UU minister and a Buddhist. Given the limits of words and concepts to explain experience, I've settled on the following way to explain it.

As a human being, I have three interdependent aspects of my nature that I struggle to understand: my religion, my spiritual practice, and my theology. I am a Unitarian Universalist in my religion; I am a Zen Buddhist in my spiritual practice; and I connect best to the school of process thought, a metaphysical sense of ongoing creation, in my theology.

Process theology lends me great hope. I believe that every moment is based on all that has ever happened and holds the potential for all that is possible. What happens in any given instant contains doors that open and doors that are closed. We stand on the threshold of all that is possible, and we are facilitators, even catalysts, for what happens next— or does not. What an awesome and awful responsibility for each of us, as agents of creation moment by moment! Who wouldn't want to be wide awake and fully alive for this? There is so much at stake! On the wall of my study hangs a large calligraphy of an *enso,* the Japanese circle symbol expressing a moment that the mind is free. Underneath, the admonition from the evening chant in our Zen liturgy: *Awaken. Take heed, do not squander your life.*

Each day as I do my work as a community minister in Roxbury, an underserved neighborhood of Boston, my spiritual practice conditions me to have a heightened awareness of my imaginary perception of what *is*. I appreciate how much of my perception and perspective arises from my social conditioning and personal life experience. I recognize much more readily my attachment or emotional stance to any outcome I'm trying to achieve in our work. My theology makes me acutely aware of my role and responsibility in the potential of the moment, as an agent of ongoing creation. I weigh my choices about influencing some action—will I make it happen, stop it from happening, or just let it happen?

Equally important as I engage in each moment is my acceptance of every other individual's participation in the same moment. I've come to appreciate that my way is not necessarily the only or right or best way. In social justice work, these aspects are extremely critical, especially in interfaith and secular settings. So many times I have heard people explain that they cannot work on an issue with those in another group because they can't accept the values and beliefs of those others. And most of the time the social need at hand is unrelated to those beliefs!

Operating from my public identity as a UU minister at work in the larger society, my Zen practice helps me stay connected with my own core theology as I work with people who have a different fundamental understanding of nature, including human nature. As I am invited to pray in an interfaith setting, I look to understand the spiritual connections to our shared work. When I am able to get beyond words, beyond the unfamiliar or what isn't true for me, I recognize the same longing for connection and meaning-making that is the root of my own impulse to devote my life to social change.

Within my Buddhist spiritual practice, I am also deeply influenced by the basic moral tenets of Buddhism, the precepts. From among the sixteen *bodhisattva* (enlightened being) precepts I lean most heavily on the three jewels, or refuges (the Buddha, the teachings, and the community), and on the three pure precepts (do not create evil, practice good, actualize good for others). I chant the three refuges, alone and with others, to remind myself of the scaffolding on which I depend for insight, wisdom, and support: "I take refuge in Buddha, I take refuge in *dharma* (teachings), I take refuge in *sangha*."

Relying on these treasures, I commit to the three pure precepts as guiding principles for my thoughts, words, and deeds: "I vow to avoid evil. I vow to practice good. I vow to save all beings." At times I feel the great weight of the injustices and systemic oppression I witness every day. Without my practice I imagine I'd be terribly discouraged; instead I am filled with hope. Trusting that countless others make these same vows daily reassures me that I am part of a much larger collective effort. It brings me a heightened sense of all the energy expended by so many individuals acting collectively to change the course of our shared future, so many choosing the way that will ultimately save us all. When I am having a particularly bad week and can least afford to devote a whole evening to sitting with my sangha, that's often exactly when sitting provides the best prescription for restoring my balance. Sitting with others who carry a similarly challenging array of responsibilities, even if completely different in content, I recognize how much my own mind is clouding my options with stress and judgment.

The ecological activist Mardy Murie once wrote to a friend, "Don't worry about what you will do next if you take one step with all the knowledge you have. With all the knowledge you have there is usually just enough light shining to show you the next step." This feels exactly right, describing a fully awakened state of trusting one's own agency in each moment as life unfurls. We sit together, and I return to center, to the moment, where all is calm and quiet.

My practice allows me to lean in—perhaps even to dive in—to social justice ministry beyond the walls of our Unitarian Universalist congregations, both in direct service and in advocacy. It allows me to be realistic and at the same time hopeful. It allows me to become aware of what people actually need and deserve, rather than what I think they need—information only acquired through deep listening and careful attention.

Awakening.
Being present.
Being fully alive.
Perfect.

—◄o►—

**CATHERINE SENGHAS** *is the senior minister and executive director of the Unitarian Universalist Urban Ministry, in the Roxbury neighborhood of Boston, Massachusetts. She is a graduate of Smith College, the University of Chicago's Graduate School of Business, and Andover Newton Theological School. Prior to entering ordained ministry, she enjoyed a twenty-year career in accounting and financial management. She also serves on the Board of the UU Buddhist Fellowship.*

# Zen and
# a Stitch of Awareness

## Marni Harmony

For the most part, identifying as a Unitarian Universalist is a matter of self-selection. Demographic studies suggest one doesn't really even need to be a member of a Unitarian Universalist church to claim affiliation. And if one does become a member, this typically involves little more than participating in some kind of new member class, signing the membership book, and making a financial pledge.

Saying one is a Buddhist can also involve self-selection; one does not have to be part of a faith community or *sangha*. But the process of becoming Buddhist includes taking the precepts (vows not to kill, lie, steal, use intoxicants, or be sexually irresponsible). Zen Buddhism requires a formal process of lay ordination called *jukai,* which involves a commitment to the basic precepts of Buddhism, regular and lengthy meditation practice, the preparation of particular documents, a willingness to honor the ancestral lineage (a transmission of teaching that traces back to the Buddha himself), and the hand sewing of a vestment called a *rakusu*.

Buddhism is said to have traveled from India to China under the guidance of a monk named Bodhidharma. Since the Chinese were suspicious of this new religion, Buddhist monks risked danger if they wore their robes. So they began the custom of creating a rakusu, a kind of mini-robe that could be hidden under a monk's clothes. The rakusu is a symbol of both commitment and liberation from fear.

After studying Buddhism for a number of years, I finally decided it was time to go a little deeper into my interest and commitment. I decided to prepare to receive jukai. My particular Buddhist lineage encourages students to follow the Zen Peacemaker Order guidelines for making a rakusu. The pieces of material that go into making the rakusu must be begged or be scraps that have been discarded and found. One does not go into a store and buy new material. I decided to seek pieces of material from people who have been important to me or who represent something significant in my life. As it turned out, all but two of the scraps were from Unitarian Universalists. Unitarian Universalism is literally woven into my rakusu.

One piece comes from my longtime dear friend Cedar. The material she offered came from a piece of robe that was given to her grandfather when he was a missionary in Turkey; a piece that reminds me of the blessing of deep friendship and the importance of sharing our faith. Another piece comes from friends Brenda and Woody—a sweat rag used when Woody was going through cancer treatment; a piece that reminds me of suffering. A piece comes from my beloved Nancy—cloth from jeans we found in a thrift shop in Scotland, reminding me how important is the love of a partner. A piece comes from another old friend, Carolyn—a portion of the curtain that hung in the back of her little truck when she traveled across the country offering a UU ministry of music—honoring the gift of her music in my life. A piece comes from my dear colleague and friend Kim, now serving as minister of the Arlington Street Church in Boston. I've known Kim since she was a teen, when I served as student minister in our church in Concord. Also, a year prior to that, I had served my first student ministry at Arlington Street. Kim sent me a piece of the old fabric that once covered the pews in that church. Both of my parents were already deceased when I was making my rakusu. To honor my maternal line, I took some homespun fabric from a trunk in my parents' attic— likely made by my maternal great-grandmother. And I have pieces of my father's pajamas—several pieces, because of his importance as one of my spiritual teachers but also because they happened to have Santa Claus on them and they remind me to lighten up! The piece of cloth sewn around the outside of the rakusu comes from the preceptor who gave me jukai, Roshi Joan Halifax, symbolizing how the teachings hold everything together. And the piece of cloth that hangs behind my neck and holds the rakusu comes from a member of the church I was serving when I sewed the rakusu, who was part of our "One Year to Live" group (based on Buddhist teacher Stephen Levine's book of the same name). It reminds me of the fragility of life as well as the importance of the beloved community.

The rakusu is worn whenever you receive teachings or are in meditation. At a Zen center, morning meditation ends with a particular chant, during which time all of us who have received jukai take our rakusus and place them on our heads. They are placed in a particular way. It's all very serious. And that's fine. Maintaining form is serious business.

During the summer that I received jukai, a brilliant and sharp-tongued woman frequently came to meditate at the Zen center where I was in residence but she did not otherwise participate. She came to one of the weekend workshops, and during one of the discussion periods she commented, "You're not going to find me sitting around with a bunch of yard goods on my head!" I laughed out loud. She was so right. Here we were, a bunch of serious, well-intentioned adults sitting around with old scraps of material on our heads. Symbolic and significant or not, it's still pretty comical. On the one hand, my rakusu reflects some of the most compelling relationships and truths of my life; on the other hand it's full of stuff you'd find at a yard sale—for really cheap!

Whenever I wear my rakusu, I am reminded to be to-tally focused on every action; to be awake and aware in the present moment. I remember the effort I made to follow the prescribed pattern—each cut and piece measuring precisely the same length in each person's rakusu. I remember the help I received from other aspirants and the help I offered them. I remember that every single stitch was done by my hand, and that I was chanting particular blessings with each one. And with every wearing, I am careful to follow the precise way of unfolding and then refolding the rakusu before putting it into its handsewn cloth envelope.

Beyond the obvious significance of my taking a deeper step into Buddhism, this rakusu is important to me as a Unitarian Universalist for several reasons. First, it suggests a disciplined path. I have found that the word *discipline* gets rather a bad rap among UUs. We often eschew the word as if it's an affront to our commitment to religious freedom. We more often speak of *spiritual practice* rather than *discipline*. *Discipline* sounds like a set of rigid rules, or at least some set of behaviors or guidelines that one is expected to adopt and follow. Or we may associate it with punishment, as in "That child needs disciplining." In any case, it's not something we typically associate with being much fun. It's a "have to" sort of thing.

Centuries ago, Aristotle wrote about character and discipline. He believed that character is shaped by forming habits of life through disciplined effort and practice as well as by cultivating morally significant friendships.

I think of discipline as something chosen by us from within rather than imposed from outside. Spiritual discipline is about making a choice. It's about choosing to open your heart rather than close it. It's really that simple. Every day offers us opportunities to choose. For me, spiritual discipline is holy connection with that which is both transcendent and grounding. I use the word *discipline* because it suggests effort and energy and deepening over time. Sometimes it has boredom associated with it; sometimes pushing yourself a little harder than you want to; sometimes choices that result in a loss of some kind. But ultimately it forms a foundation for deepening awareness. Discipline provides some structure in the wide world of choices offered by Unitarian Universalism.

Secondly, my rakusu is a constant reminder that I have roots in a long lineage and must strive to honor the practice of my predecessors. That is equally true for my roots in Unitarianism and Universalism. As we sing in one of our precious hymns, "what they dreamed be ours to do, hope their hopes, and seal them true."

Finally, my rakusu serves as symbol and reminder of why I'm part of a UU congregation. The various pieces of fabric come together in a rakusu, just as we Unitarian Universalists are challenged—through both discomfort and joy—to create community out of diversity.

My rakusu suggested to me the image of a "yard sale." Many UU congregations hold annual yard sales—the time when we receive whatever anybody is ready to discard and willing to donate. We're generally undiscriminating when it comes to donated goods. You brought it; we'll take it.

There may be a few boundaries, such as please don't bring toxic waste; don't dump old appliances that don't work anymore; make sure the clothes you bring are clean; don't bring puzzles that have missing pieces. But generally we receive whatever shows up.

Unitarian Universalism is a yard sale religion. We bring our lovingly used but very best china and our lovingly used but very best recipes, our imperfect but lovingly broken-in best selves and our imperfect but lovingly developed best truths, and we share them with our community. Yard sale religion may be filled with hand-me-downs and leftovers and frayed fabric, but their meaning and purpose are clearly identified. When I go to a yard sale, I don't try to find something that I can then turn around and re-sell. Rather, I hope that I might find just exactly the right little something. Likewise, I hope that when people check out our yard sale religion, they will find just the treasure they've been looking for—the idea, the vision, the relationship, the understanding that brings something that was missing but deeply needed in their lives. At our theological yard sale, we have UU Christians, humanists, Buddhists, Earth-centered pagans, naturalists, mystics, and agnostics. We have those who embrace liberation theologies, feminist theologies, process theology, and so on. These, then, are the theological threads and yard goods we have to offer. It's a pretty rich yard sale, if you ask me. And sometimes a scrap is exactly what someone needs to open his heart or transform her life.

My rakusu symbolizes both spiritual freedom and discipline. It's a bunch of scraps representing diverse lives and sewn together with effort and love. It reminds me every day to be aware and intentional, to live with joy, to seek clarity as I embrace the interdependence of the ten thousand things. It reminds me to be guided every day by my truest sense of purpose: I'm a seeker of meaning. I have deep things yet to learn. May I be a simple, humble, kind presence on earth today. May I do no harm. May my actions reflect my deepest beliefs.

◄○►

**MARNI KYOJU HARMONY** *has served congregations in State College, Pennsylvania; Brookfield, Wisconsin; Orlando, Florida; Marietta, Georgia; and Tarpon Springs, Florida. She received lay ordination in the Zen tradition in 2001. She credits her father, her partner Nancy, her dog Gus, and friend Sensei Irene Kyojo Bakker as her greatest Zen teachers. She still tries to live up to the honor of both ordinations.*

# Do Good, Good Comes

## Ren Brumfield

**A** sign proclaiming, "One Church, Many Paths" greeted us as we entered West Shore Unitarian Universalist Church in Rocky River, Ohio. I wasn't sure if the many paths could include mine. For the previous six years, the path I walked had led me to a Vietnamese Theravadan Buddhist teacher and temple. Now I was in a new city, in search of a spiritual home that I could share with my partner, Dawn. I was grieving the loss of the physical presence of my teacher in my life, and of the community of the temple where he taught.

Arriving in the Cleveland area, Dawn and I had explored the Buddhist temples and did not find anything that felt like what I had experienced at Chua Buu Mon in Port Arthur, Texas. We had a Buddhist friend back in Texas who was also a member of Spindletop Unitarian Church in Beaumont. At her suggestion, we decided to visit West Shore Unitarian Universalist Church.

We walked in to a beautiful, modern space with art on the walls and a bright rotunda filled with people who seemed genuinely happy to be there and to be in each other's company. On our first Sunday the church was having a service connected to a Jubilee World weekend of anti-racism anti-oppression training. West Shore was celebrating the diversity of the UU faith and of its own community. As had been the case at most of the Buddhist temples in Texas, there were not many faces in the crowd that looked like mine, but everyone made us feel welcomed. The members of the church made us feel like we were part of the family. That was a large part of our decision to join.

Church had been part of my life growing up because of my grandmother's involvement in her African-American Baptist congregation. I returned to my home state of Texas in the late 1990s with a wife and a young daughter and remained unaffiliated with any church. By 2000 I was divorced and left trying to figure out what to do. I was twenty-nine years old and newly estranged from my ex-wife and my child. Alone in my new apartment, I rediscovered the library of Buddhist books that I had been collecting since college. I had owned these books for some time, but in the mental space I occupied before the divorce, they were not speaking to me. I was beginning a new journey into the world and into my own mind.

I sat with the Zen writings of the contemporary Vietnamese teacher Thich Nhat Hanh and the twelfth-century Japanese Zen innovator Dogen Zenji. I took a literary journey from death to rebirth through the *bardos* (transitional states of being) described by the ancient Tibetans, and fled from Tibet to India with the fourteenth Dalai Lama. I imagined sitting in a Southeast Asian forest, one of many monks listening to the wise words of the Theravadan teacher Ajahn Chah. The story of Prince Siddartha Gautama (the historic Buddha) now seemed much more accessible, given my present situation.

I decided that I needed to personally experience the teachings of the Buddha, since I had come to know about them only through books and since these words had held my interest since my teenage years.

Houston has a sizeable Asian population. I had become familiar with a small part of it in years prior, when I was learning Mandarin in college. Through the Internet, I found that the Jade Buddha Temple, a Chinese Pure Land temple, in the southwest part of town, had an "English Dharma Group" that met on Sunday mornings. After some procrastination, I attended my first meeting.

Dragonflies skimmed over a large, lily-filled pond at the foot of a statue of the Buddha of Compassion, Kwan-Yin near the temple's main entrance. The woody and spicy aroma of incense wafted from an ornate pot near a group of people practicing tai chi. I followed signs to where the English Dharma Group held its weekly meditations and talks. I was early. I met the Venerable Hung-I Shih, one of the senior monks. He was a small, bespectacled man, who wore a yellow robe and white leggings and had a friendly smile.

As would be the case with most of the monks I came to meet, there was a presence about him that was quiet and calm but at the same time powerful and humbling. He was born in Burma, moved to China at a young age, and had been a Buddhist monk for most of his life. We spent time talking, just the two of us, before the group began. I was very comfortable with him because he seemed like someone from whom I could learn a world of things. I told him how I had come to be in that place at that time and about my desire to dive more deeply into Buddhist and Chinese cultures.

I didn't have much money then to donate to the temple, but I had decided that I would contribute my time and energy wherever I could in exchange for what I sought. I volunteered to help move furniture and to serve food. I helped decorate for events and painted faces at carnivals. Early on I was asked to represent the temple at an interfaith Thanksgiving ceremony at the Rothko Chapel in the city's museum district. Eventually, through the English Dharma Group, I had the opportunity to lead a class or two on the basics of Buddhism for newcomers.

One day the Venerable Hung-I asked me for a favor. Without question or hesitation, I answered yes. He asked me to be a substitute teacher for a kids' Buddhism class in the temple's Chinese school. I was honored to be asked but feared that my knowledge of Buddhism was inadequate and that my Chinese only rudimentary. Yet Venerable Hung-I's confidence in me was powerful. At the last minute, the class didn't happen, but I still have the two illustrated bilingual books that he gave me that day.

During my time with the Jade Buddha Temple, I had many opportunities to travel the Houston area and visit temples and to get to know monks from Chinese, Korean, Vietnamese, Laotian, Cambodian, Thai, Sri Lankan, and Tibetan traditions. I treasured each cup of tea, each shared meal, each time we would sit and chant verses from the Buddhist canon, and each opportunity to discuss the *dharma,* the teachings of the Buddha.

After about a year at the Jade Buddha Temple, my job took me a hundred miles away, to my hometown of Beaumont, Texas. Not long after the move, around the time of the December celebration of the birth, enlightenment, and death of the Buddha, I returned to the temple to participate in a lay ordination. I donned a brown robe very similar to the ones worn by the monks, and in a ceremony full of drums and bells and chanting, after countless bows and prostrations, I took the precepts to formally become a Buddhist practitioner. As is tradition, each of us that were ordained that day was given a dharma name. The family name given to all of us was Zhi, which translates to "Wisdom." My individual given name was Ren. I didn't know how I felt about it when I got it, because it sounds much like my own English name. Written in Chinese, it combines the characters for *knife* and *heart* and is commonly translated as "tolerance," but it carries a meaning closer to "self-control" and "self-restraint." After a little time getting to know it, it seemed right. It was Ren redefined.

The Beaumont area was home to many Vietnamese who had come to the United States as refugees in the mid to late 1970s. Some of them founded Chua Buu Mon (Beaumont Buddhist Temple). In the 1980s the Buu Mon Buddhist Association bought an old Catholic church in Port Arthur, transformed the steeple into a tower, and relocated there. Growing up in Beaumont and having gone to Port Arthur numerous times, I had never really paid attention to the place. Now that I was back, I realized that it wasn't enough for me to make the occasional trip back to Houston to participate in Buddhist temple life. I wanted to find a new, and closer, Buddhist "church home."

Eventually, I visited the temple in Port Arthur. When I did, there was only one monk in residence, the Venerable Thich Huyen Viet. He was often out working in the gardens during the day, which is why I usually could not get him when I had tried to call.

I joined the Venerable Huyen Viet for green tea in the lunchroom outside the temple's office. At that time, there was not much programming for people who did not speak Vietnamese. But by then I spoke a few words of the language and Venerable Huyen Viet spoke English, and what I wanted then was to be part of a Buddhist community as I had been at the Jade Buddha Temple in Houston.

Having been given an open invitation to drop by after that first visit, I would go to Chua Buu Mon several times a week, in the afternoon, and take photographs in the gardens. When the light faded in the evening, I would sit in the lunchroom with "Thay" (Vietnamese for "Teacher"), as I had come to call Venerable Huyen Viet. We drank green tea while I shared the photos from previous visits with him, or we watched the evening news. Often, he invited me to stay for dinner, which was prepared by Ba Cu (Grandmother), the elderly woman whom I had earlier attempted to speak with on the telephone.

As we became more familiar, Thay would call me to let me know when events were going to happen at the temple and ask whether I would be coming to photograph them. Soon I was responsible for the bulletin board in the temple's main hallway.

Before long I would occasionally be asked to proofread letters written in English that were sent out from the temple. Eventually, I began writing temple correspondence, which evolved into a part-time job a few days each week. Thay called me "Monk's assistant." The title alternated, depending on the task at hand or with whom we were speaking. As "Temple's Public Relations Officer," I worked with radio, TV, and print journalists, and my friends in the local artist community to get the word out about public events. I reached out to other clergy in the area, inviting them to be Thay's holiday guests at Lunar New Year, and Vesak celebrations. In return, we were invited to be guests of the rabbi of the local reformed synagogue or of the bishop of the Catholic diocese at their public celebrations.

It was the best job I ever had. In one day I got to speak Vietnamese with members of the temple; introduce curious Americans to Buddhism, the temple, and Vietnamese culture; speak Chinese with visitors; and speak Spanish with the men who would sometimes help Thay work in the garden.

Thay had a saying that summarized his philosophy and, in my opinion, all of Buddhism: "Do good, good come." I gave much of myself to the temple, but I received so much more. I spent the next four years driving the twenty miles there from my home as often as I could. I had a small room upstairs in the monk's quarters where I occasionally spent the night. I had access to the temple's library of Buddhist books. Thay would humor all of my questions about the Buddha's teachings, and I would explain American idioms to him. We would discuss life and the world while we dug in the stinky muck when it was time to refresh the soil in the lotus ponds.

We had one such conversation when I told him that I was in love with a woman from Cleveland whom I had met several months before, and that I wanted to move there to be closer to her. We were both a little sad that it was time for me to leave the temple and the father-son/master-student relationship we had developed, but I had to do it. The weekend before I left for Ohio, Dawn, the woman I would eventually marry, took a weekend trip to Austin with Thay for the Texas Bamboo Festival. We spent my last night in Texas at Chua Buu Mon. In the morning, we ate breakfast with Thay, lit incense, bowed to the Buddha in the sanctuary, and said good-bye.

I won't pretend that my experience of becoming a Unitarian Universalist at West Shore Church has been anything like developing this master-student relationship with a teacher in a community that became my home. One of the ministers at West Shore is a Buddhist practitioner who has received the precepts. That was an encouraging connection and it has provided some continuity as we entered the church, but he practices in a Zen tradition, which doesn't attract me. More importantly, West Shore has offered me a sense of community and the ability to be just who I am within it.

Over the past few years, I have been a member of our Diversity Change Team and have gone to the Ohio Meadville District Assembly. I have been a member of the Queer and Allies Group. I have worked closely with our intern ministers. Being a member of the Worship Associates Team was probably the most challenging, and the most rewarding of my experiences at West Shore. Getting to know the co-ministers, Wayne and Kathleen, researching sermon topics and finding readings and helping to set the order of service reminded me of what I had done in the temple before I moved to Ohio.

Together, Dawn and I were now in a position where we could contribute financially to the church, but for us the true connection to the community is how we serve it. We were married at West Shore in October of 2010. This year, 2012, my daughter, Amber, has come to live with us in our new house, and I have been elected to serve on the church's Board of Trustees.

My path continues to be my own, and it has become one of the many paths that comprise our one church at West Shore. I continue to hear Thay's voice telling me that if we continue to strive to do good, certainly good will continue to come to us. I find ways within my Unitarian Universalist community to realize this truth day after day, year after year.

—◄o►—

**REN BRUMFIELD** *is originally from Beaumont, Texas, and is a student of Theravada Buddhism. He and his family joined West Shore Unitarian Universalist Church in Rocky River, Ohio, in 2008.*

# Taming the Elephants in the Room

## Alex Holt

**D**runks are sometimes depicted as seeing pink elephants after one too many.

I had elephants, too. They weren't pink but usually blue to match my mood. I had a whole herd of them in the living room of my life. They even had names. One was "alcoholism." Another was "deep craving for a good relationship." A third was "confusion," especially about what it meant to be a parish minister. There were others, too. A special one was "calling myself Buddhist" without really knowing what that meant.

It was sometime after Easter 1994, and I was living in Oregon. I had essentially moved into my office after leaving the home in which my wife and her son lived. My extension ministry position had been much harder than I expected, and I was distracted by alcohol and the struggles in my marriage of less than two years.

The herd of elephants that stomped around before me needed to be tamed, or at least fenced in, but I didn't know what to do. The good folks at the UUA Department of Ministry had advised me to take a sabbatical from ministry to look at my addiction, my marriage, and my ministry. More importantly, they hoped I would explore the causes of the conditions that resulted in these raging elephants of delusion, visible not only to me but to anyone with eyes to see.

I had not come from any traditional religious background. Buddhism had appealed to me for many years, but mostly through reading books. Unitarian Universalism felt like home because I could reject dogma and Christian exclusivism in the company of kindred spirits. Then it all hit the fan in 1994. In this crisis of faith, I couldn't find a spiritual practice of discernment in the religion I loved. It's easy for religious authorities to say, "Take a time of discernment," without offering any options. Where was I supposed to look within my faith for support and guidance?

Then I remembered the Sources. I had somewhat stubbornly told people in churches and seminary that the six Sources of Unitarian Universalism—which describe the sources of our religious inspiration—were far more important than the seven Principles—which describe the values we affirm as an association of congregations. I remembered a discussion some years earlier where I told a UUA official, "We don't get to pick which Sources we like and ignore the rest. They're all the same package." Maybe the Sources would help me corral the elephants and make them stop their insistent noise.

I looked up the Sources once again. They contained some powerful hints about the fence I needed to build for my elephants: "direct experience" and "words and deeds of prophetic women and men." There was "wisdom from the world's religions which inspires us in our ethical and spiritual life." And there was "humanist teachings which counsel us to heed the guidance of reason." In that moment I saw them all pointing me in the direction of Buddhism and its teachings of direct experience, steady attention, and getting to the bottom of cravings.

A month later I was sitting in my office reading the ads in the local alternative weekly paper. A Buddhist retreat center in Washington State needed a facilities manager. I thought to myself "Aha, a sign of where I need to go." I applied for the job and was hired despite dubious qualifications. All was now in place: Move there, get sober, have good therapy, and enter dharma practice! It would be easy!

But my craving mind had other ideas. I struggled with drinking on-and-off because others at the center drank, too. I had lusted after at least one female staffer. I developed a resistance to daily meditation, because it was expected of staff. My self-centered and adolescent stubbornness continued.

I met my Zen teachers a year later at the retreat center. I asked them to accept me at their new training monastery in Oregon. I neglected to mention my elephants, the ones that were now inside a fence but pushing at the gate.

I went to the Zen monastery and loved the people and the challenges. It wasn't easy. I still drank in secret, though I had worked through some important childhood and life issues regarding my romantic and sexual relationships. Dharma practice flowed through me. I eagerly grabbed on to the sixteen precepts especially those that warned against stealing, lying, and becoming intoxicated.

I'd had no previous authentic spiritual practice of contemplation, prayer, or retreat in my UU religious faith. Zen wasn't simple, but it had a simple instruction. I summarized it in a phrase that Zen teacher and UU minister James Ishmael Ford has used in his blog: "Meditation in the Zen tradition really boils down to three things. Sit down. Shut up. Pay attention." What an essential addition to my Unitarian Universalist approach to faith!

"Sit down" had never been a theme in my training as a minister or in my congregations. To Zen practitioners, sitting down meant taking the one seat of meditation and preparing to be still. Do most Unitarian Universalists take that time every day, or weekly, or even annually? Do we stop our hurrying to seek to heal the world and hear our causes speak to us? It seemed to me that we were addicted to action rather than reflection.

To "shut up" means to stop the ceaseless questions we bring to the world. The old bumper sticker "To Question is the Answer" is only half the truth of Unitarian Universalism. The other half is "to live the questions" themselves, to paraphrase Rainer Maria Rilke advising the young poet.

Shutting up a Unitarian Universalist in meditation means to look inward at the deeper reasons we ask questions, resent authority, and push back against traditions.

"Pay attention" asks us to be aware of what is going on in our hurry-up-do-something minds. What are the causes of our conditioned responses to traditional religious language? Paying attention requires us to discern the emotional as well as the rational attributes of life.

So my Zen teachers and others patiently and mostly gently held up a mirror for me to examine myself. Was I slowing down, becoming more thoughtful about life and my vocation? Was I moving beyond delusions that were driven by ego? Why was I losing myself in alcohol or sexual craving? What was I avoiding?

When I left the monastery I did so because I couldn't quite tame that last big elephant of addictive craving for the next drink. It kept escaping the enclosure, mostly because I kept the gate unlocked. Delusions of the mind are pretty smart, in a sneaky sort of way.

It kept getting out until June 14, 2003. On that day I decided it needed to be penned up once and for all. I knew for certain now that I needed help to do that, so I went to Alcoholics Anonymous meetings. I talked with fellow Buddhists in recovery. Most importantly, I admitted I couldn't do it by myself.

I've thought about what finally happened to turn the corner to sobriety. Was there a connection between UU values and dharma teachings that helped me? The first Unitarian Universalist Principle asks us to honor the inherent worth and dignity of every person. Buddhism reminds us that compassion and loving-kindness must begin with us. In *Kindness, Clarity, and Insight*, the Dalai Lama wrote, "If in day-to-day life you lead a good life, honestly, with love, with compassion, with less selfishness, then automatically it will lead to [awakening]."

In my first days of authentic sobriety, I had to become honest with myself, with my partner Debra, with my Zen teachers, with my congregation at the time, and with my fellow addicts in recovery at AA. This is why the first of the Twelve Steps is so important in any discernment or spiritual deepening: We admit we are powerless over [our addiction]—that our lives have become unmanageable.

My tribe of recovering alcoholics understood that and supported me unconditionally. My other tribe of fellow Unitarian Universalists truly lived the first Principle, and held up for me the light of my own worth and dignity, even though there was confusion about how to help me. A third community of dharma teachers, students, and fellow practitioners were sympathetic and caring, although it seemed that only the fellow addicts-in-recovery could speak beyond dharma dogma.

My recovery from addiction continued, despite the challenges of a serious car accident and pain medications. It continued despite the post-traumatic stress syndrome brought about by that accident and my early life.

*Karma*, the law of cause and effect with intention, continued to unfold. I was asked in 2005 to initiate a Pacific

Northwest District Addictions Ministry team. Later I was invited to Chicago to collaborate with colleagues and laypeople about the best courses of action when ministers relapsed or struggled with addiction.

Still later, I helped to found and support the first UUA Addictions Ministry program. That led to the discovery of a very similar program started among Buddhist dharma teachers and students. Addiction and craving, as Buddhist teacher Kevin Griffin would write, was "desire gone mad," wherever it appears.

So my own cycle of karma and intention moved on, from the desperate pleasure of the first drink to the authentic pleasure of recovery and service to others.

There's one other lesson to learn from my twin faiths of Buddhism and Unitarian Universalism. The former historically has focused more on individual awakening and less on the healing of the world. The latter has for many years gazed outward, to bring sanity and wholeness to the world beyond our skin. Each tradition has its strengths and weaknesses.

As a UU immersed in alcoholism, I found no place in my faith to tame those elephants in my living room, because they were actually inside me. Our faith seemed to have no doorway for inner work. Buddhism supplied an answer but in the end, didn't seem to give me any clear option for service to others.

Together, they have fulfilled the spirit of the Twelve-Step model despite its many flaws. To heal, we must sit down, shut up, pay attention, and to listen to the voices beyond our skin. To serve others, we must move beyond our rugged individualism and navel gazing.

Now, eighteen years after that Easter in 1994, I still revere the Sources and speak of them as the fundamental container of Unitarian Universalism. I now recognize my elephants in the room as the "three poisons" of greed, anger, and ignorance that the Buddha named. They have been tamed, or at least downsized. They'd love to get out of the pen I keep them in, and lead me over the nearest cliff. I stay alert for their presence.

Now I proudly hold up the dharma of recovery as a loving relationship between the Sources of Unitarian Universalism and the teachings of an extraordinary teacher and his entire lineage. Every time I hear or chant the lines found in the Zen liturgical poem "The Identity of Relative and Absolute," they remind me there are no elephants and no pen. Just practice and service.

—◦—

**ALEX HOLT** *is a long-time Zen student associated with Chozen and Hogen Bays of Great Vow Zen Monastery in Oregon. He is a specialist in advanced interim ministry and is interim minister in Bend, Oregon, after serving many other congregations. He is in his tenth year of sobriety and continues work with the Buddhist Recovery Network, the UUA Addictions Ministry, and Faith Partners, Inc. out of Austin, Texas.*

# Zen to UU and Back Again

## David Dae An Rynick

When we moved to Worcester, Massachusetts, in 1991, my wife and I were already practicing Zen Buddhists. This nontraditional affiliation made our initial forays into friendship somewhat awkward. At one dinner party we were insistently invited to attend a local synagogue. Only after persistent questioning did we confess to being Zen Buddhists. This was "polite company." And though everyone tried to hide their surprise, being a Zen Buddhist was clearly a conversation stopper.

With no Zen community in town, our social isolation and longing for spiritual community eventually led us to church shopping. Our first stop was First Unitarian on Main Street. We were headed for mainline Protestant churches, and this was first on our list because a new friend had told us they had good music. Upon our first visit, we found this to be gloriously true. But more importantly, our first worship service included a unison reading of a

T. S. Eliot poem and a sermon that began with a traditional Zen story. Halfway through the service, my wife, Melissa Blacker, leaned over to me and said, "This is a spiritually correct place."

After the service we "came out" to the senior minister as Zen practitioners. She was delighted and told us of her own meditation practice. We knew we had found a home, and we officially joined the church several months later.

Those early days of attending First Unitarian are still vivid. Aside from our Zen community in Connecticut, which was decidedly countercultural, I had never been in an institution where people were encouraged to speak openly of their spiritual journeys. Yet Sunday after Sunday, our minister spoke of the possibilities and challenges of our journey toward the sacred. She drew from many wisdom traditions but clearly spoke with the voice of experience. She never told us what we should believe but encouraged us all to follow our own minds and hearts.

First Unitarian in Worcester, Massachusetts, was gathered in 1785 and is a grand old New England church on Main Street, between the courthouse and the largest Methodist church in town. Though UUs may be regarded as countercultural in some locations, in Worcester they were clearly part of the mainstream establishment. I remember being surprised that the well-dressed, normal looking people sitting around me were interested in these kinds of services too. This was my first inkling that my spiritual journey might be a public part of my life as an adult.

A year or so after our arrival, we were asked to lead a two-session introduction to Zen meditation. When we received an enthusiastic response to those sessions, we were asked to begin a weekly Zen meditation group. We had already been leading a nonsectarian meditation group in the family room of our house, but this was our first foray into our emerging roles as Zen teachers. Both of us had received informal permission to teach from our respective Zen teachers, but First Unitarian gave us the space, the encouragement, and the "customers" to take this important step in the journey that has eventually led to our becoming fully authorized Zen teachers.

We were also invited to serve on committees and participate in the church leadership. While my wife quickly realized that this was not where she wanted to contribute to the church, for me, these invitations opened a doorway that was enticing and fun. At last I could use my professional skills to support and grow an organization that was concerned with matters at the very heart of being human.

As an eager and at least moderately competent volunteer, I quickly ascended through the ranks and, after six or seven years, became moderator (president) of the Prudential Committee (the governing board). In that role, I worked closely with the minister to clarify and support the mission and vision of our church. The work of being a lay leader both challenged and supported me to find my voice and to learn how to stay focused on the essentials in the midst of all kinds of distractions. Being received and encouraged as a leader was part of a fundamental shift in how I saw myself and what was possible for me in the world. The skills and capacities I gained at First Unitarian have been essential in the task I later took on to help create a new Zen Buddhist religious community.

Meanwhile, my wife and I continued our study and practice of Zen. We worked closely with several different teachers and regularly attended retreats. The weekly Zen group at the church continued, and a weekly group that met at our home attracted more and more people. Eventually we had to clear all the furniture out of our living room to accommodate the number of people attending.

After my tour of duty as moderator, I became less active in the leadership of the church. This happened partly because I was literally burned out (we had a fire in our sanctuary!) and partly because I was pursuing a new career as a life and leadership coach. However, there was an even deeper current drawing me away from active engagement in Unitarian Universalism. While both Zen and Unitarian Universalism are noncreedal religions that privilege individual experience as the ultimate source of authority, the differences between the two traditions became increasingly apparent to me.

Zen Buddhism is a path with clear disciplines. This ancient tradition, inherited from Japan and Korea, requires a commitment to a regular practice of meditation, both on one's own and in the presence of community while on retreats. While reading and discussion can be useful, they are not enough to be considered a practicing Zen student.

The other essential aspect of Zen training is a personal relationship with an authorized teacher. Both my wife and I were fortunate to have Zen teachers who supported and guided us in traveling deeper into this ordinary mystery of being human. Through these ongoing relationships and through our growing community of students and fellow practitioners, we continued to identify more deeply with the path and the tradition of Zen. Over the past several years, we each completed our formal training to become Zen teachers.

As this went on, we met and eventually joined forces with James Ishmael Ford—a UU minister and Zen teacher. Together, we started Boundless Way Zen, an association of Zen groups throughout New England and beyond. Like the sitting group we began in Worcester, many Boundless Way groups have had their origins in UU churches. As we became more organized we started leading residential retreats together, attracting more and more people. On the day that forty people showed up at our house for a day-long meditation retreat, we knew that we needed a larger space.

In the summer of 2009, my wife and I took a great leap of faith. We sold our lovely home of twenty years and bought a large rambling Victorian house that we immediately dubbed Boundless Way Temple. Since that time we have led daily Zen meditation sessions and periodic residential retreats. We are the resident teachers and we are organized as a 501c3 religious nonprofit organization.

We have a Temple Leadership Committee (TLC) that looks surprisingly like a Prudential Committee. We have membership and pledges, committees and task forces. We are a full-fledged religious institution.

While we are still members of First Unitarian, we now have very little contact with the day-to-day operations of the church. Our transition to fuller commitment to the path of Zen coincided with the retirement of our dear friend and minister, Barbara Merritt. With this personal connection gone, we remain on friendly terms with the current minister but don't feel the same heart connection as we felt with Merritt.

I still work with UU congregations and clergy as coach, workshop leader, and occasional preacher, but my wife and I are clear that our primary religious identification is as Zen teachers and practitioners. Nevertheless, we continue to feel deeply aligned with the values of Unitarian Universalism that support and honor the individual religious journeys of all. Boundless Way Zen continues to have close relationships with several UU churches. And a number of the members of our temple remain actively involved members at First Unitarian and find that the combination of the religious paths serves them quite well.

I don't see our drifting away from active engagement in a UU congregation as a sign of failure on the part of Unitarian Universalism but rather evidence of one of the important roles our UU communities can play—as a place where people can feel at home, be accepted for who they are, and be encouraged to follow what is most true for them, whatever form that may take.

First Unitarian was exactly what we needed when we came to Worcester. It allowed us to be ourselves and encouraged us to honor our own experience and to follow our own path. It led us to a deeper and more primary engagement with Zen Buddhism—a great credit to the liberal religious tradition of Unitarian Universalism.

—◦—

**DAVID DAE AN RYNICK, ROSHI** *is the abbot of the Boundless Way Zen Temple in Worcester, Massachusetts, where he lives and teaches with his wife, Melissa Myozen Blacker. He is a long-time Unitarian Universalist and member of First Unitarian Church in Worcester. In addition to being a life and leadership coach, he is also the author of* This Truth Never Fails: A Zen Memoir in Four Seasons, *published by Wisdom Publications.*

# Longing to Belong

## Joyce Reeves

**W**hile I am not currently a member of a Unitarian Universalist congregation, I was a very active participant for most of the 1970s and 1980s and still consider myself a UU. Part of what drew me to Unitarian Universalism was freedom from a creed that I could not embrace. I was asked only to honor my spiritual path and to respect the diversity of beliefs and practices the community represented. I appreciated being with other socially and politically active people who valued nature and human dignity. But I was in a scientific community where Unitarians tended to be heady—to err on the side of intellectualism, mental constructs, principles, and ideas. While I could not fault the content or the social action, it often felt disconnected from feeling and deep mystery—essentially the heart—so there was little lifeblood for me.

While training as a Gestalt therapist, I became deeply involved with the inner life, with the mystery of dreams and fantasies, with the longings that rule the human heart, and especially with the depth of denied feelings that make up the undercurrents of most people's lives. I came to trust the truth of the expression "The only way out is through." In this type of therapy, the work focuses on accepting and trusting whatever emerges in the moment as meaningful or useful, including so-called forbidden feelings. As my training and practice as a psychotherapist evolved and as I explored other, more spiritual practices, I found myself longing for something deeper than my UU congregation could offer. I experimented with shamanism; Buddhist, Hindu, Sufi, and other forms of chanting and meditation; nature-based practices; sacred site travel; vision quests; and more. I trained with some extraordinary teachers, including Joan Halifax, Jean Houston, Angeles Arrien, and Robbie Gass.

I first learned of Joanna Macy, Buddhist scholar, systems thinker, and deep ecologist, during an Open Heart Therapy workshop designed by Robbie Gass. At one point in the workshop, we were asked to lie on the floor in a large circle, close our eyes, and stay present to our feelings as the most horrendous sound track invaded every cell of our bodies: guns, bombs, sirens, screams, chaos. I will never forget the rawness of that experience. We were being trained to be present to horror and suffering. This exercise came from the work of Joanna Macy. At the time I knew only that she had written a book called *Despair and Personal Power in the Nuclear Age.* Only years later did I experience her work directly.

My first workshop with Macy was everything a searcher like me could wish for. "The Work That Reconnects" did just what it promised. I reconnected with my spiritual longing, my strong love of nature, and my desire to make a difference. The glue for this work seemed to be Macy's clear and abiding belief in the mystery and beauty of the interconnectedness of all of life. The unique combination of experiential exercises, opportunities to connect with other participants in meaningful ways, and deep inner practices felt powerful and completely in sync with my therapy training and practice. It was as though I had come home to a new place where the rooms contained parts of my being, with nothing left out. And there were new rooms to explore, including Buddhist systems thinking and practices.

I was not a complete stranger to Buddhism, having explored meditation practices over the years. And I had happily uncovered some very insightful Tibetan Buddhist practices I could use in my work. "Feeding Your Demons," as taught by Tibetan Buddhist nun and teacher Tsultrim Allione, offered a brilliant means of dealing with fear, by inviting the "demon" to present itself clearly, discovering what it wants and giving it whatever it desires. For example, if the fear demon indicated that it wanted the person's happiness, happiness would be offered up, but only from the great source of all happiness, not from the individual. After a few minutes, the demon would be satisfied and slowly disappear, taking the fear along with it. This is an oversimplification of the practice, but it worked consistently and fit beautifully with Gestalt therapy.

*Tonglen* is another powerful Tibetan Buddhist practice that I have used personally and professionally for many years. At its heart is the opportunity to be generous, to be willing to breathe in suffering and breathe out comfort—whether for oneself, another person, a situation, or the planet. What I find so compelling about this practice, similar to "Feeding Your Demons," is the willingness to take in the so-called negative and give away any goodness. It seems counterintuitive and is generally counter to Western thought, which largely promotes breathing out any so-called negative emotion or feeling and breathing in the positive. Yet tonglen offers a deep sense of freedom from fear of loss or contamination. It instills trust that what rides in on the breath can ride out on the breath.

"Breathing Through" is a meditation Macy adapted from Buddhist tradition. It offers a way to be open and fully present to the full catastrophe of the social, political, and environmental crises facing our planet. In recent years as I offer workshops based on Macy's teachings, I often teach this practice in preparation for the despair segment of the workshop. Like tonglen, it supports breathing in specific concerns, carrying them on the breath through the heart—this is a crucial part of the meditation—and sending them out of the heart into the great heart of the world, into the vast web of life. Nothing to avoid or dismiss.

Each workshop strengthens my sense of the rightness and the timeliness of coming together to our connection to the largeness of life, to the living earth, to ancestors and future beings. This is heart work, and it takes guts. These workshops move through a spiral from "Gratitude" to "Feeling Our Pain for the World," to "Seeing with New Eyes," and ending with "Going Forth."

By all accounts, the despair segment, "Feeling Our Pain for the World," is the most powerful and meaningful of Macy's work, and it is the part I find missing in nearly all social action groups, including UU congregations. It is indeed rare to have a safe place to fully feel and express the true depth of fear, anger, grief, and emptiness that lives just beneath the surface of our lives. I frequently hear people comment that they can no longer listen to the news, that they feel powerless against the big corporations' control of government, that thinking and feeling about what we know is happening to our environment is too overwhelming. The list is as endless as the wars in which we are engaged. It would be so easy to drop out, to carry on as if nothing is happening. And this might be a wise choice if it were the only alternative.

With a solid foundation in gratitude, Macy's work invites the rare opportunity to allow feelings to fully flow in the presence of witnesses. In the space that follows, love blooms and becomes the ground from which action then naturally takes place. We want to save what we love. It's almost that simple. Generosity can then flow. It was shocking and deeply moving to me to have that first workshop end with a practice called "Bowing to Our Adversaries." I wept with every statement, each of which basically revealed that the people and practices we love to hate really reveal what we truly love. We would not be so outraged and aggrieved if we did not love so deeply. Thanking corporations for waking us up may seem like a big stretch, but it is good to stretch our minds and hearts if the end result is an activism motivated by love.

Recently, I was invited—with my co-facilitator—to present a daylong workshop of "The Work That Reconnects" at my former UU meeting house. What an extraordinary experience! We presented in a room that was once the main sanctuary, where I had actively participated in leading services, performed in a play, listened to countless sermons, and sat on the Board. Several of the participants in the workshop were members of the congregation I knew so many years ago. I was reminded of what I loved about being a Unitarian Universalist and what made it so challenging at times. When a workshop participant stated that he had never really made eye contact with another member of the congregation, I was confronted with a familiar dilemma. I wondered whether we can feel deeply connected to ourselves and others when we only focus on the leader (preacher). I wondered whether coffee hours, committee meetings, and lunches with the minister support continuing dialogue or deep connection. I wondered whether extra-church activities generated safety and belonging but not necessarily spiritual growth.

The church group seemed to have difficulty with the despair experience, often expressing more thoughts than feelings. I considered whether this response had anything to do with Unitarian Universalism and the people it attracts, or whether the fact that many participants knew each other well and must face each other regularly was the more significant reason. Of course, there is always the possibility that we did not present the exercise effectively. Above all, I wonder why I care. Probably because I still think of myself as a UU and I want to believe that this rich tradition can hold the breadth and depth of experience I've come to expect.

I feel perfectly at home with Unitarian Universalist beliefs, language, rituals, politics, and ethics, and I cherish this. Yet in Unitarian Universalism I miss the depth of inner work that is offered by Buddhist and other traditions. Recently I have taken weekend trainings in the Shambhala tradition—a blend of Tibetan Buddhist lineages founded for the West by Chogyam Trungpa Rinpoche. The trainings are offered by a wonderfully openhearted, artistic, and socially conscious community. I have some difficulty with this form of meditation and don't begin to understand its depth of teachings, traditions, language, and rituals. Yet I value the level of self-exploration that ultimately supports social action.

Creating workshops with members of the Interhelp Network—an international organization begun by Joanna Macy and others in the 1980s—is certainly gratifying and helps to fill this need. The annual weekend workshop I attend, The Work That Reconnects, is a great model for shared leadership and community building. Still, I find myself longing to be in ongoing community with like-minded souls who want to go deeper and who are willing to create the trust and safety that it entails. And while I haven't belonged to any congregation for a very long time—over twenty years—this return to my old UU meeting house felt like coming full circle in some mysterious way.

◄○►

**JOYCE REEVES** *is semi-retired after more than thirty years as a psychotherapist and workshop facilitator. She is a budding Buddhist and a Unitarian Universalist at heart and has been a long time advocate for peace, social justice, and environmental stewardship. She currently serves on the Council of the Interhelp Network, a volunteer organization dedicated to furthering the teachings of Joanna Macy.*

# REFLECTIONS

# LOVING-KINDNESS

## KIM K. CRAWFORD HARVIE

At the beginning of a six-day meditation retreat led by all-star Buddhist teachers and authors Sylvia Boorstein, Sharon Salzberg, and Joseph Goldstein, we take a vow of silence. Additionally, we vow not to read, write, or look at one another; we will spend the next six days at the Insight Meditation Society in Barre, Massachusetts, sleeping, eating, and meditating with seventy-five people, engaging with no one but ourselves. But this is no solitary venture. The intention of the retreat is, in essence, to put Unitarian Universalism's seventh Principle—affirming Unitarian Universalists' respect for the interdependent web of all existence—into action, to connect me in a profound way to every other person in the meditation hall, and far beyond.

On the first night, Sylvia Boorstein instructs us in memorizing four simple phrases, translated from the ancient Burmese language Pali. The phrases say:

May you be free of danger.

May you have mental happiness.

May you have physical happiness.

May you have ease of well-being.

These are the *metta* phrases, the practice of generating loving-kindness, a twenty-five hundred-year-old gift from the Buddha, the awakened one. "Saying metta," one does nothing more—and nothing less—than silently repeat these four phrases. I am told that a Tibetan nun, imprisoned by the Chinese government, survived torture and solitary confinement on the knowledge that somewhere in the world, in every moment, someone, somewhere, was saying metta for her and her jailers. I'm all in.

The wake-up gong sounds at 5:15 a.m. Seated meditation begins at 5:45; at 6:30, it's time for breakfast. Breakfast is followed by an hour of walking meditation. And then it's back to sitting. Day after day is just this: seated meditation, followed by walking meditation, until the final evening sitting ends at 10 p.m. And the metta phrases, over and over and over. The routine is punctuated only by a one-hour talk by one of the retreat leaders each evening; a two-hour work period, for which my assignment is to help in washing the lunch dishes; light meals; and using the bathroom.

I am a student of Zen Buddhism; this *vipassana* (insight) practice is new to me. I feel, at times, as though I were in prison, especially at night in the large, open room I share with sixteen other women. At other times I feel like I'm in the back ward of a psychiatric hospital, as we all shuffle around with our eyes averted: meditation, or medication? This is Joseph Goldstein's image; in one of his evening talks, he says, "In a way, you are in a mental hospital. And your mind is getting better."

The retreat begins with sending metta to yourself: "May I be free of danger; may I have mental happiness; may I have physical happiness; may I have ease of well-being." You progress from yourself to a living benefactor—a teacher or spiritual guide for whom you feel respect and gratitude— and send metta to them. Next, you choose what is called a "neutral" person—a person you don't really know, about whom you have formed no passions or dispassions—and send metta to them: "May you be free of danger; may you have mental happiness; may you have physical happiness; may you have ease of well-being." Sharon Salzberg says it is important to approach increasingly difficult people gradually. High-wire metta is naming your enemy—the literal translation from Pali is your "difficult person"—and send metta to them. Finally, you send metta to all beings—every being who has ever lived, is living, or ever will live. When you have it down, the entire sequence runs in a continuous loop. And then it's the sixth day, and time to go out into your real life again. Six days wholly devoted to cultivating loving-kindness!

This is the story of the second morning. We have been meditating for perhaps two hours when we are instructed to choose a living benefactor, a teacher for whom we feel gratitude, and to send them metta. The first person who surfaces in my quiet mind is my mother, a single parent to my younger sister, Lisa, and me. This is a surprise; our relationship has not been uncomplicated.

I'm sitting on my meditation cushion, absolutely still, and my mind begins to wander. Do I really want to spend this entire day with whatever might come up about my mother?

No, and yes.

If I'm really going to make something of this retreat—if I'm really going to experience something transformative and wake up—is there any other living benefactor whom I might invoke at this time?

Yes, and no.

My mother has grand mal epilepsy. As I sit there in the early morning light with my yes-no hanging in the wintry air of the meditation hall, the woman behind me falls to the floor in a familiar thud: a seizure.

As a half dozen of us leave our cushions to help, I realize for the first time the kind of chronic fear my mother must have felt throughout my childhood: When she seized at home, there was no one to help her but a child. The compassion I feel opens up the possibility of connecting with her at a deeper place, deeper than our personalities. As deep, perhaps, as her soul.

Mum, may you be free of danger.

May you have mental happiness.

May you have physical happiness.

Mum, may you live with ease of well-being.

Two days later, it is time to send metta to our enemy, our difficult person. Having devoted so many productive hours to my mother, it seems only right to spend a day with what might surface about my father. I don't wait for a sign, but start right in. I am after that expansive vision, that liberation of the heart promised by the Buddha's awakening.

It is not easy. I spend much of the morning making deals with myself: For every five, "Dad, may you be free of dangers," I get to do one for my daughters. During three periods of walking meditation, I choose to go running, giving me the illusion of getting through the metta phrases faster. I make up a little running meditation tune, a little metta tune, which turns into a metta symphony. Anything for distraction. I am silent, but it's noisy inside my head.

Glancing at my watch, I notice the date and realize, with a jolt, that this is an anniversary: It is twenty-seven years to the day since my father walked out on our family. Twenty-seven years! A long time to bear a burden of grief and despair and anger, a burden that serves no one. Suddenly, it's the perfect time to lay that burden down.

And then, out of the blue, it comes to me that my daughter Jamie is exactly the age Lisa had been when our father left. Six years old: innocent, guileless, open and tender hearted. In my mind's eye, I see Jamie, I see the little Lisa, and the question arises, Who could abandon such a child?

Just as quickly, the answer comes: only someone who is very, very sick. Soul-sick.

With this understanding, loving-kindness floods my heart, and I feel an outpouring of compassion, the release promised by the awakened one.

Dad, may you be free of danger.

May you have mental happiness.

May you have physical happiness.

Dad, may you have ease of well-being.

The heart sees clearly. To truly wish someone well is to see them with our heart, and so experience a change of heart—a transformation not in them but in our relationship to them and in ourselves.

No matter where our path leads, beyond all our suffering, beneath all our changes, we are, at the deep heart's core, unfragmented and undivided. Awakened to this wholeness, whole and holy, there is no such thing as a stranger or an enemy. To truly wish someone well is to make of our lives a peaceful and joyous place. All of our homing instincts call us there. And it is not far away—not far at all.

May you be free of danger.

May you have mental happiness.

May you have physical happiness.

May you have ease of well-being.

—<o>—

**KIM K. CRAWFORD HARVIE** *is a fourth-generation Unitarian Universalist and has served as senior minister at Boston's Arlington Street Church since 1989. She has practiced Zen Buddhism since the late 1970s and studied religion in Japan. Having raised three daughters, she and her wife, Kem Morehead, a teacher at Concord Academy, are houseparents for twenty-eight teenagers, living across the street from Henry David Thoreau's childhood home.*

# Four Impossible Things Before Breakfast

## Wayne Arnason

Every morning after I do my Zen meditation practice, I vow to do four impossible things before I have my breakfast and go to work at the Unitarian Universalist church where I serve as co-minister. The four impossible things include saving all beings, extinguishing all delusions, mastering all opportunities to realize the Buddha's teachings, and embodying fully the Buddha's way of being. Somehow, after reciting these vows, the challenges of the day look less daunting! They are at least put into perspective.

These four impossible things are the Great Vows, which in different languages and in different translations within different languages are chanted around the world in Buddhist communities and monasteries at least once every day. Here's one version:

"Beings are numberless, I vow to save them,

"Delusions are inexhaustible, I vow to end them,

"Dharma gates are boundless, I vow to enter them,

"The Buddha Way is unsurpassable, I vow to embody it."

Sometimes I will look at myself, sitting cross legged and chanting in monotone about these four impossible things before breakfast and marvel that this is me, a midwestern Canadian born-and-bred Unitarian Universalist who serves as a minister in our tradition. How did I get here? Is this spiritual? What benefit do I get from focusing on these vows? Are these the right questions to be asking about them? My personal perspectives on these questions about the Great Vows may offer some understanding of why many Unitarian Universalists are attracted to practicing Buddhism in some form.

Studying Buddhism with a teacher can be a little like talking to Carnac the Magnificent, the character comedian Johnny Carson created for *The Tonight Show*. Carnac would hold an envelope with an unknown question inside it. He would place the card to his forehead and announce the answer before opening the envelope and revealing the question. Knowing the answer first, the question is the surprise. When the question is revealed, we all get to laugh, and that's the reward.

In Buddhism, the answers are pretty much all out there in the liturgies, the academic books, the poems and sutras, and in the conversations and talks from an authorized teacher. Nothing is hidden. Knowing the questions that need to be asked about yourself is much more difficult.

So here's one answer to why I promise to accomplish four impossible things before I eat my breakfast: All of these impossible things that I vow to do are impossible because they are already done. All things are interconnected and interdependent. That's why sentient beings are already saved. That's why delusions have ended. That's why the *dharmas* are already entered. That's why the Buddha way has already been embodied. So if that's the answer, what I am really asking here?

The question is, What stands in the way of realizing this truth since it cannot be "gotten" or "earned"? Here the word *realize* needs some unpacking. In conventional speaking, we use this word to mean "understand," as in the sentence, "I had trouble following the sermon at first but then I realized what it was all about." But the *realize* used in Buddhist teaching means more than just following a line of argument or learning something new. It very literally means what the word itself implies: "to make real." Ideas about enlightenment, about how the world works, about what spiritual practice is supposed to do are ultimately just ideas. They are only part of what we need to live our lives with joy, equanimity, and integrity, while remaining aware of our interdependence. When you make a teaching real, it means that you have consumed it, absorbed it, made it part of your whole body and mind. Realizing the teaching is "being the teaching," not just understanding

the teaching and reciting it back to yourself or to a teacher
or to a *sangha*.

One of the members of the congregation I serve likes to say
that the shortest and best definition of Unitarian Universalism
is "deeds not creeds." This resonates with the Buddhist invitation to realize the teachings in everyday life. Throughout my
life as a Unitarian Universalist, I have felt the challenge of our
faith tradition to act on what I say I believe. That action has
included being a supporting member of a church wherever I
lived, and responding to invitations to leadership and service.
Unitarian Universalism has never been an intellectual exercise
for me. It is a way of living in the world. When I found Buddhist teachings and practices, it was easy to understand that
the tradition was challenging me to move beyond reading
books or trying out meditation practices.

The first step that I took to meet this challenge was
to look for a teacher. Not all Buddhist communities in
America invite or require this kind of relationship, but it
was the right next step for me in making my Buddhism
real. I believed a trusted teacher could coach, encourage,
and correct me in the process of making the vows I chanted
into something more than words.

The children's book *The Velveteen Rabbit* by Margery
Williams offers an important clue about the Buddhist definition of *real*. The Skin Horse's advice to that Rabbit about
becoming real is that "it doesn't happen all at once."

Making real, or realizing, the Great Vows doesn't happen
all at once either, and it doesn't happen in the same way,

at the same pace, or even through the same process for everyone. Even though the central teachings of Buddhism are the same all over the world, Buddhism takes many diverse forms, and each person who practices it follows a different path. This is particularly true in the Zen school, which holds that enlightenment is realizing the mind of the Buddha as something available to and inherent in everybody, passed on outside the formal learning found in the scriptures. The tradition uses the word *awakening* to describe what can be a very short or a very long process of making real the inherent *Buddha nature*, or essential being, that is within us.

No story in Buddhism provides a stronger reminder of how all people must find their own realization, their own way to enlightenment, than the story of Gautama Buddha's two most famous disciples, Mahakayashapa and Ananda. Mahakayashapa was a relative novice when he first encountered the Buddha, but there was apparently a powerful connection between them. When they first met and made eye contact, the Buddha moved over to make room for Mahakayashapa on his cushion. Tradition says that in eight days of study Mahakayashapa attained his first experience of awakening. Around this time, the Buddha was preaching from the top of a small mountain called Vulture Peak. At one point in his sermon, the Buddha held up a lotus flower and twirled it in his hand to illustrate a point. He looked toward Mahakayashapa, who was in the crowd that day, and their eyes met. The Buddha blinked.

Mahakayashapa gave back an almost imperceptible smile. What happened in that moment? I don't really know. The story reminds me of Malcolm Gladwell's stories about tipping points—moments of equilibrium that are reached and then passed where there is enough energy, enough will, enough openness, enough courage for an individual, a community, or a country to step into a new way of being. Mahakayashapa had done just that. The Buddha saw it and came over to Mahakayashapa and, to the surprise of all, gave Mahakayashapa his robe and bowl, saying, "This wonderful *dharma door* that establishes no texts and is a special transmission outside the scriptures, I entrust to Mahakayashapa." The Buddha had essentially designated Mahakayashapa as his successor teacher, because he recognized that Mahakayashapa had the same mind as the Buddha and had realized his true nature. Mahakayashapa was in this way recognized by the assembly and since then has been called The First Ancestor.

Now if you were Ananda, you might imagine that this would be hard to take. Ananda was actually a cousin of the Buddha. He was born on the same day that the Buddha attained enlightenment. His name means "happiness and joy." When he was of appropriate age, he became a student of the Buddha and served as his attendant. He spent the most time of anyone with the Buddha. He was a brilliant man, with an amazing mind and a photographic memory. He listened to every word that the Buddha said over twenty years, and he committed the Buddha's sermons to memory.

The Buddha described him as foremost in learning and gave him much approval and respect. If there was anyone that people expected to become the Buddha's successor after his death, it was bound to be Ananda. Ananada saw the Buddha twirl his flower and blink that day. But Ananda didn't get it. Whatever was recognized or made real in that moment didn't happen for Ananada.

Ananda continued in his service to the Buddha, and when the Buddha died, Ananda became Mahakayashapa's attendent for twenty more years. Mahakayashapa asked him to help communicate the teachings. He would often ask Ananda to recite to the Assembly what the Buddha had said, and everyone agreed that he could do so impeccably. But the transmission of the light, that tipping point, where the teachings all came together and were realized within and without you, had never happened for Ananda.

Finally, one day after these twenty years of learning and service with Mahakayashapa, Ananda felt compelled to ask him a question that had been nagging him. "Master," he said, "When Buddha gave you the robe and bowl, did he give you anything else?" Mahakayashapa looked at him, and replied, "Ananada."

"Yes, master."

"Take down the flagpole at the gate."

In that moment, Ananda reached his tipping point. The flagpole at the gate was used in monastic communities as a sign that the teacher was giving a talk, was expounding the dharma. When the flag was lowered, the talk was over.

Mahakayashapa said to Ananada, "Take down the flagpole. Not only is the teaching over, you need no flagpole to raise any more flags ever again."

I've always felt more akin to Ananda than to Mahakayashapa—one of those plodders who is really good at absorbing the teachings and giving them back, but slow and steady in making them real. That's why I wanted to become a formal Buddhist student, receive the Buddhist precepts or ethical teachings, and recite the vows every day. It's like raising the flag every morning. It's a reminder that there is teaching about to take place as the day unfolds that can help me realize some things I know intellectually to be true, but that I haven't absorbed into my whole body and mind quite yet.

"Beings are numberless. I vow to save them" says the first of the Great Vows. Save them from what? How? If they are numberless, infinite, how can I save them all? Intellectually, the answer is that I am saving them from greed, anger, and ignorance—the roots of our suffering—and that to do so, I need to recognize that there is no barrier, no difference between me and the rest of the world that comprises every other being. I can never save any of them if I cannot save myself first from greed, anger, and ignorance. So I start with myself. The first and greatest contribution, perhaps the only contribution I can make to saving all beings from their suffering is to realize and act on the causes of suffering in myself.

I find this insight and vow to be a good antidote to the admirable intensity I see in many fellow Unitarian Universalists who are committed to saving the world "out there" but who are ill equipped spiritually to do this without suffering personal burnout and disappointment as the endless tasks produce disappointing results.

"Delusions are inexhaustible, I vow to end them." For many years I actually chanted a different translation of this vow, one that uses the word *desires* instead of *delusions.*[*] Ending desires was a pretty tall order. Pass the cookies, please. Sure, I'll have another drink! Desires are indeed inexhaustible, and for me at least, ending all desire is going to take something drastic, like death. I needed to approach this particular impossible task in a different way. Intellectually, I understand the question to this answer to be "Can you end one desire at a time?" If everything is interconnected and interdependent, and if the present moment contains the whole universe, then dealing with the desire that is in my head right now is really all I can do anyway. When the next desire comes up, then that will be the one to deal with, but not now.

Delusions similarly come up one at a time, but they are all manifestations of one great delusion that underlies it all and that I remember when I recite this vow. That one great delusion is that there is something permanent in this world to hold on to. As a tradition hospitable to and deeply influenced by humanism, Unitarian Universalism has always

---

[*] English translations of Buddhist texts can vary considerably. There is no one "correct" version, and being aware of the various translations can help us to better understand the text or chant.

been comfortable with letting go of God as a guarantor of anything. My theist UU friends usually hold God lightly in their embrace and never use the creator they love as a weapon against others. Buddhism's nontheistic approach challenges humanists and theists alike to look at the ideas of the universe they may hold dear or take for granted as things that are useful, but insubstantial. Buddhism also challenges each of us to look at the idea we have about our "selves" as permanent and solid fixtures of reality. When we consider that there is no self, we look at the passing parade of experiences and our long train of memories in a very different way.

Ending delusion connects with the simple practice that is involved in meditation, which is noticing the impermanence of everything that comes up while just sitting, and learning to do just one thing at one time.

"Dharma gates are boundless, I vow to enter them." *Dharma* means two things at the same time: It is the teaching of the Buddha, but it is also the opportunity that exists in every moment to apply the teachings to the present moment of experience—so every moment is a gateway to realizing the teachings. For me, this vow resonates with the Unitarian Universalist conviction that the most important life is the one we are living right now and that heaven and hell are created by human beings right now. When I remember the "dharma gates" and seek to enter them every day, I can see that there is no need to worry about mastering all the teachings of Buddhism or behaving in some enlightened way in some future moment. There is only this moment to be in and to realize how greed, anger, and ignorance get in the way of experiencing it without any separation or barriers between me and what is in front of me. If I can engage with this moment without attachments, the teachings that are the dharma take care of themselves, and all the dharma gates open at the same time.

Finally, the last of the Great Vows says, "The Buddha Way is unsurpassable, I vow to embody it." The word *embody* addresses what it means to make real the teachings with the whole body and mind. Another translation of this vow puts this issue more starkly and paradoxically, however: "The Buddha Way is unattainable! I vow to attain it!" In the paradox of vowing what seems impossible, we return to a key issue in Buddhist practice, represented by this word *attain*, and the answer to the question that the Zen Master Carnac the Magnificent will always offer: All things are connected and interdependent. The Buddha Way is in fact unattainable, because there's nothing to attain. You already have everything you need. You just don't know it or can't see it. That's why practicing together with others and having a relationship with a teacher is so important— because through and with others you increasingly begin to see what realization looks like in practice, and you begin to recognize the places in yourself where your experience and behavior is different because you are embodying the Buddha Way. Whether it happens quickly, as with Mahakayashapa, or slowly, as with Ananada, is not as important as the fact that it does happen and it will happen, as you remain committed to the practice.

In this one life we know we live—the life that poet Mary Oliver calls "wild and precious"—we have an opportunity to embody a practical, nondoctrinal, insightful way of being in the world. Nothing about the Great Vows and how they call me to live my life contradicts my lifelong identity as a Unitarian Universalist. Rather, the Great Vows complement that identity, and challenge me to make real my UU practice. I see realizing my life as a Unitarian Universalist and a Buddhist as an endless task. There's no schedule, no expectation that I will ever be done. It doesn't matter whether I am more like Mahakayashapa or Ananda. What matters is that I receive the gift of my wild and precious life and enter it fully.

"Take heed," chants a student at the end of each day of an intensive meditation retreat, "Take heed, do not squander your life!" As I begin my days with four impossible things, I take this advice to heart. I go on to the next thing—to chopping the fruit salad or shaving my face. I enter that gate completely, and in doing so, find the whole universe on the other side.

◄○►

**WAYNE TONJIN ARNASON** *is co-minister of West Shore Unitarian Universalist Church in Rocky River, Ohio, with his wife, Kathleen Rolenz. He has been president of the UU Buddhist Fellowship, and has also served as president of the UU*

*Ministers Association and as chair of the Ministerial Fellowship Committee. He began meditating in 1970 and has been a Zen Buddhist student since 1995.*

# FROM DEFICIT TO ABUNDANCE

## SAM TRUMBORE

**B**uddhism is gradually working as an influence within Unitarian Universalism so that the two traditions are knitting together in a mutually affirming way. Buddhism is also guiding the evolution of our own unique method of spiritual practice. Those of us who grew up Unitarian Universalist and have many years of mindfulness practice are leading the way, through our own direct experience.

After serving as minister of the First Unitarian Universalist Society of Albany, New York, for six years, my congregation granted me a six-month sabbatical that began January 1, 2006. Not losing a precious moment of time, I began my sabbatical with a two-week self-guided meditation retreat at the Insight Meditation Society Forest Refuge in Barre, Massachusetts. The Forest Refuge is a beautiful modern retreat center set back from the road in a grove of trees. It is designed for long and very quiet retreats with the minimum of disruption. Evening inspirational sermons called *dharma* talks are spaced three or four days apart. Guidance sessions with a teacher are similiarly spaced. The quietness of the halls and grounds, particularly in winter, makes a pin-drop rattle the nerves. The center has been designed to facilitate the development of *samadhi* and *sati*, of concentration and remembering-mindfulness.

In this quiet, peaceful setting, my concentration strengthened and my awareness sharpened. As I settled into the silence at the beginning of the retreat, I often experienced discomfort and distress as my mind resisted slowing and calming down. Transitioning from the fast pace of the Christmas season to watching the snowflakes forming gentle piles on a statue of the Buddha easily caused intense moments of restlessness. And sometimes this agitation manifested itself as upsurges of old emotional pain and trauma.

The primary emotion that dominated me as I sat motionless wrapped in wool blankets watching my breath come in and go out was the feeling of not being good enough. The deep roots of this feeling have no beginning in my memory. On my first-grade report card, Mrs. Logan wrote with concern how hard I was on myself as I tried to do everything right. My father wrote back that he also observed this in my personality and that he and my mother were working on it with me at home. Whatever they did, it didn't work. I've been inwardly driven to achieve perfection my whole life. The price of that striving, even when I consciously let myself be more relaxed, has been self-judgment.

I always wanted to be as smart as my parents, who seemed absolutely brilliant to my young, impressionable mind. My father taught physical chemistry at the University of Delaware, where my mother also worked, in the reference department of the library. I could ask any possible question, and my mother could find the resources that would supply an answer. At the dinner table, I'd ask a scientific question. A smile would appear on my father's lips. He would bring out a pen from his pocket protector, open up a napkin on the table, and begin to reveal the great truths of science to me. I remember looking with awe at the complex formulas of integrals and differential equations he worked with to describe wave patterns generated by ionizing radiation of water, wondering if I could ever be smart enough to comprehend his life work.

In middle school, I developed a chronic intestinal condition that slowed me down from following my father's example and becoming a scientist. The pain and discomfort disrupted my concentration and clarity of thinking. Not that I didn't do well in high school and college—far from it. The intestinal condition made me feel like I wasn't good enough to achieve the intellectual greatness I so highly prized.

Great suffering results from disconnection. My response to this disconnection was to try harder, to compensate for any weakness. If I couldn't be a great scientist, let me graduate from a prestigious university, get a high-paying job, climb the ladder of opportunity, make a lot of money, and achieve a successful life.

And a good life I have had, I thought, as I brought my attention back to my right foot gently lifting off the ground, ready to move and then place itself in the walking meditation path I was slowly wearing into the floor. Happily married with a thirteen-year-old son, serving a thriving UU congregation, living in a nice home, and in reasonably good health, I had nothing to complain about. Yet thoughts of sermons that could have gone better, calls that I forgot to make, less-than-soothing visits with troubled parishioners tormented me. Would this sabbatical turn me into the excellent minister I wanted to be, the one who could satisfy every member and gradually bring them all to awakening and liberation?

I don't remember the exact moment that the conviction came into my mind. When it did, I felt a tremendous sense of relief and release. The thought arose: *I am* good enough already. Nothing has to change, I don't need to learn one more skill or experience anything else—*right now* I am good enough.

Immediately my mind began leaping to make connections. The first connection was to the first Principle of Unitarian Universalism: "inherent worth and dignity of every person." I wondered if before this moment I had really believed it about myself. Yes, I could easily see the inherent worth and dignity in the members of my congregation and in my family, but I knew the contents of my mind too well. I could see the judgment, anger, and fear creating a barrier to my feeling of self-worth. In a moment of clarity,

I understood that my unwholesome mind states could not extinguish the light of love in my heart. That light had a source independent of what was happening in my head.

American Universalist founder Hosea Ballou saw our uncertainty about God's love and our fear of eternal torment as the sources of our misery. For Ballou, the penitent sinner asks, "Will my actions alienate my creator so that I will be cast down into the fire?" The trouble is not with a loving God but with the worried sinner. Ballou found the message of love again and again in the life of Jesus. God's unconditional, unlimited love for all of us endlessly overcomes our conditioned and limited sin. That Universalist vision of irresistible salvation, in the words of contemporary UU minister Rob Hardies, "would not let me go, let me down, or let me off."

Nineteenth-century Unitarian minister James Freeman Clarke, in his 1886 essay, "The Five Points of Calvinism and the Five Points of the New Theology," offered a different view of salvation than his orthodox contemporaries:

This salvation has been explained as some thing outside of us,— some outward gift, some outward condition, place, or circumstance. We speak of going to heaven, as if we could be made happy solely by being put in a happy place. But the true heaven, the only heaven which Jesus knew, is a state of the soul. It is inward goodness. It is Christ found within. It is the love of God in the heart, going out into the life and character. The first words which Jesus spoke indicated this belief. The poor in spirit already possess the kingdom of heaven. The pure in heart already see God. "This is life eternal, to know thee, the only true God, and Jesus Christ whom thou hast sent." He who has the faith which Jesus possessed has eternal life abiding in him. The water that Jesus gives becomes a spring of water within the soul, "springing up into everlasting life." Do not look for a distant heaven, saying, "Lo! here," or "Lo! there"; "for the kingdom of heaven is now with you.

My mind jumped to the connection with Buddhism. We *all* have Buddha nature. Could this "faith which Jesus possessed" be equivalent to Buddha nature? Even the murderer Angulimala, who vowed to kill a thousand people and cut a finger off each to make a necklace and who attempts to kill his final victim, the Buddha, can awaken to his capacity for wisdom and compassion and find liberation. No matter what we have done or had done to us, nothing can cancel out this life-giving property of existence. The stressful mental response to the unsettled and unsatisfactory qualities of existence can come to an end. The difficulties of existence that cannot be overcome do not limit our ability to know an inner peace, equanimity, and tranquility that is unconditional and full of loving-kindness.

Knowing that I can realize my Buddha nature is a little like learning to juggle eight balls. Yes, I know it is possible, because I've seen people do it. I've seen people like the Dalai Lama and recognize their ability to manifest their

Buddha nature. But how in the world do I get there? And as a minister, how can I lead others to that state of bliss?

The first three of the four noble truths of Buddhism would be incomplete without the fourth. The first unpleasant truth states that the impermanence of all that exists causes the unenlightened mind a lot of distress. The second unpleasant truth describes the three ways we react to that distress: by clinging to what we like, rejecting what we dislike, and wandering in confusion. The third truth is much, much more pleasant. This experience of distress can come to an end. The fourth truth is the path of liberation from stress, called the eight-fold path.

Knowing that we can achieve liberation is useless without the marvelous eight-fold path that prepares the way for awakening. By applying our energy to developing mental clarity through concentration and mindfulness, we cultivate the wisdom to recognize and understand the arising of clinging, rejecting, and ignorance and to decide what intentions are worthy of translating into speech, action, and economic activity.

I redirected my attention back to the spoon in my hand, ready to go down into the bowl for another mouthful of miso soup, and I continued to ponder. How different is the eight-fold path from the development of character, the hallmark of early Unitarianism in New England? Isn't the striving for personal moral development central to Unitarian Universalism today? Don't we educate ourselves to use the moral wisdom we develop to guide our public and private lives in seeking a better world for all? Isn't there a strong compatibility between these two real-world approaches for personal and social improvement?

The oracle of character development for Unitarians is our American founder, William Ellery Channing. He saw a nobility in the human mind that his contemporaries did not. "God," wrote Channing, "is another name for human intelligence raised above all error and imperfection, and extended to all possible truth." For Channing, the intellectual search brought us into communion with truth. As he wrote in his essay "Self-Culture,"

> Intellectual culture consists not chiefly, as many are apt to think, in accumulating information, though this is important, but in building up a force of thought which may be turned at will on any subjects on which we are called to pass judgment. This force is manifested in the concentration of the attention; in accurate, penetrating observation; in reducing complex subjects to their elements; in diving beneath the effect to the cause; in detecting the more subtle differences and resemblances of things; in reading the future in the present; and especially in rising from particular facts to general laws or universal truths.

The parallels here between self-culture and Buddhism are striking. Channing's valuing of the development of concentration and "penetrating observation" are similar to the Buddha's valuing of concentration and mindfulness.

Channing's pursuit of general law and universal truth parallels the Buddha's encouragement to discover universal truth in our direct experience. Both Channing and the Buddha had great confidence in the power of human intelligence to discern truth, a power that could be cultivated and developed through study and practice. Though they had vastly different methods and techniques, both revered the capacity of the human mind to discern truth directly, without mediation or revelation.

As a birthright Unitarian Universalist, I drank in a commitment to personal and social improvement with my mother's milk. At the January retreat, I noticed a shift taking place in my striving, which had always been driven by the goal of some day being good enough. I would only be acceptable to myself and others if I attained some ever-broadening and deepening level of competence. Suddenly I recognized the impossibility of this goal. I could not find the self-worth I sought through achievement.

I already had what I was looking for. I was already good enough. My mother and father didn't see me for the first time and think, "Some day our child will amount to something." They were overwhelmed witnessing the Spirit of Life unfolding before them. But as a newborn infant, my capacity to express my Buddha nature was quite limited. Yet as I grew, and throughout my life until my last breath, I could get better at allowing that Spirit of Life to unfold through my life in ways that benefit myself and others.

I'm good enough and can get better.

That unfolding of the Spirit of Life never stops. Even when I'm oblivious to the grand and mysterious workings of that Spirit, the folding and unfolding continues. The Buddha nature, the Spirit of Life, is working through me in each moment. The eight-fold path as well as the development of character through seeking truth and meaning can help me—and all of us—begin to recognize and understand what allows us to manifest our true nature and what can block it.

There is great fullness in the emptiness of the meditation hall at 3:00 in the morning. Sitting motionless under the unwavering eye of the Buddha, I felt deeply thankful for the abundance of my life and the opportunities I have to share that abundance. I am not some defective, fallen creature, pleading for a sign of acceptability and begging for a divine pass to some heavenly realm. I am identical with the Spirit of Life exploring the infinite field of possibility for each new moment. There is no separation to be overcome, no barrier to break through, only an abundant living truth to fully embrace and allow to work through me to guide my actions.

This abundant Spirit of Life, beyond reduction or containment or even categorization, is not Buddhist, Christian, Jewish, Hindu, or Unitarian Universalist. All can point to it but never lay claim to it. Perhaps this is the genius and potential of what Unitarian Universalism can be—honoring and appreciating the many different traditions that proclaim the greatness of that which is beyond us. Seeking the widest possible path to truth and meaning may actually enhance our ability to dive deep into the spiritual practices of each tradition without being caught by the limits of overreaching dogma, authoritarian institutionalism, and historically bound revelations.

The task for those of us who identify as both Unitarian Universalist and Buddhist is to discover the wealth of understanding and insight each tradition reveals, resisting the temptation to limit our understanding to one or the other. Each enshrines great truths that can shed light on the other. Moving beyond our divisions with a spirit of inquiry and appreciation will help us awaken and live in the presence of the great abundance of being.

I came home from my retreat more fully a Buddhist *and* more fully a Unitarian Universalist. I'm richer for their conversation within me. The vast abundance of the Spirit of Life is much clearer when seen through multiple lenses.

# THRIVING IN DIFFICULT TIMES

## DOUG KRAFT

Imagine a pre-human ancestor—a furry, lemur-like creature living furtively in the primeval forest. He sees something desirable—food or a potential sexual partner. A wired-in instinct focuses all his attention on it and prepares his body to move toward it. Then he sees something undesirable—a predator. The primal instinct focuses all faculties of the pre-human on it and prepares his body to get out of there. This instinct gives him an evolutionary advantage. This instinct is the opposite of introspection: It directs attention "out there" rather than "in here."

We humans have such an instinct. It is fast, simple, pre-verbal, nonconceptual, directs attention away from itself, and narrows the scope of awareness to the object. We have many names for it: desire, attraction, attachment, craving, dislike, fear, anger, disgust, uptightness. It's the feeling that generates the thought, "I like it" or "I don't like it," "I want more" or "Get me outta here."

The instinct is pre-cognitive and arises so fast that we can't control it. It just happens. It arises uninvited out of our neural wiring. We might describe it as "getting triggered," "having my buttons pushed," or "getting hooked in."

In the earliest Buddhist texts it is called *tanhā*—the second of the four noble truths—which says the root of our experience of difficulty is this instinctual tightening. The third truth says we can release it and know well-being regardless of our circumstances. We can thrive, even in difficult times.

How do we get there? How do we navigate rough waters in ways that quiet our minds and open our hearts? Thriving, like peace of mind, is an inner quality rather than an outward action. I believe that releasing tanhā—this inner tightening—is the key.

Tanhā is difficult to see because it directs our focus away from itself. To better understand it, we have to begin by simply recognizing the tightening itself. Then we must look at what triggers it. And finally we have to look at the most crucial aspect: releasing it and relaxing, until our lives feel enriched even during hard times.

Searching for this instinctual tightening is like my sons searching for Easter eggs when they were little. They'd run out into the yard and look under flowerpots, beneath rocks, and behind wooden boxes and find nothing. My wife and I would hide the eggs in plain sight: a yellow egg in a bed of yellow flowers, a brown egg on the root of a tree, a green egg in a tuft of grass. The colored eggs were visible but placed where they'd blend in with the yard. In their excitement, my boys overlooked the obvious. But once they learned they were in plain sight, they stopped, looked more carefully, and began to see them everywhere.

The instinctual tightening is like that—it's in plain sight, but its nature diverts our attention away from it. However, when we stop and look carefully, we begin to see it everywhere:

- A car swerves in front of you. Your hands tighten on the wheel.

- You're in a gentle, free-flowing conversation with a friend. Then her eyes cloud over and she turns away. "Did I say something wrong?" you ask. She responds curtly, "No. But I have to go!" You've witnessed the unnamed tightening in her.

- You approach the grocery checkout lines with a dozen items in your cart. All the lines are long except one. A woman with an overflowing cart heads toward the short line. Your body tightens slightly as your pace picks up.

- The Dali Lama describes being driven from a hotel in Los Angeles to a conference center. Each day the route takes him past blocks of electronic stores. He says, "Looking out the car window I want things without even knowing what they are." He is feeling tanha.

This tightening feels like an urge, a drive, or a tug. It's uncomfortable. It gets our attention by creating tension and pushing us to do something. If there's nothing to do, we're left with an edginess begging for resolution.

The instinct may help in situations that resolve quickly. It's less help in complex, nuanced modern life. By narrowing our attention, we can get hooked on a detail rather than seeing the broader context. To some degree, this instinct colors much of human experience.

So what are the triggers? There are many. Some are obvious: relationship breakdown, job insecurity, disease, death of a loved one, children's difficulties, economic insecurity, political inanity, war. Some are less obvious: loneliness, annoyance, quiet worries, loss of meaning, purposelessness, yearning for something. What do we do about these?

The tightening focuses our attention outward. Sometimes this is wise. Our Unitarian Universalist tradition emphasizes dealing with the world, not withdrawing from it. We're not monastics. We embrace the interdependent web of all life. We like to deal with issues on their own terms when we can.

If we're sick or injured, rather than just hoping and praying, we go to a doctor or health care worker or consider diet, rest, or exercise. If our job is in trouble, we to talk to the boss, send out our resume, advance our education, network. If a relationship is on the skids, we talk to the other person, consult with a wise friend, find a counselor, seek a support group.

If this resolves the problem, great. We cure the disease, find a new job, resolve our kid's obstreperousness, buy the music we wanted, and find some way to resolve the problem triggering the discomfort.

But there are times when there's no solution. We do what we can, but the difficulty lingers.

When I first moved from Massachusetts to Sacramento, California, a dozen years ago, my youngest son, Damon, was about to start his senior year in the charter high school he'd helped found and had poured his heart into. So he and my wife stayed in Massachusetts that year. I came out alone.

Mostly it was okay. I missed them, but I was busy getting to know a new congregation, and I knew the separation from my family was temporary. Still, Friday nights were hard. Fridays had been family time: We played board games, went to movies, or just hung out together. So as the twilight settled in on Fridays, my chest ached. I talked to my family on the phone. But that wasn't the same. Sometimes the pangs of loneliness seemed intolerable.

Some difficulties resist being fixed. The disease may not have a cure. There may be no jobs around. We may not have the power to solve the political scene. The loved one who died isn't coming back. Our child's problems have no easy resolution.

What do we do then?

There are three popular strategies for dealing with un-solvable problems: Grab something, push something away, or space out. Let's look at each.

The first strategy is to grasp for things, or become needy. Unresolved tightening can feel like hunger, thirst, or empti-ness. We look for something to fill that void.

When I broke up with a girlfriend in college, I was upset

and didn't know what to do. So I bought the Simon and Garfunkel album *Bridge Over Troubled Waters*. It comforted me. Many people shop to feel better. Or they look for experiences to distract them. When I was in Sacramento that first year, sometimes I went to a movie to get through an empty evening. A variant of this strategy is getting other people to do things for us. We try to control others as a way to handle our inner discomfort. Sometimes this strategy soothes us. We relax. But if it doesn't address the true hunger, it has no lasting benefit.

The second strategy for coping with intractable problems is the opposite: Rather than grasp for things or experiences, we push them away. We become irritable or angry. We've all seen this in others and felt it ourselves. We snap at people more easily, become less tolerant of foibles, lose our temper, criticize more readily. Things that used to roll off our backs now get to us. Expressing this irritability may bleed off some of the tension. But if it doesn't solve the real problem, it doesn't lead us to well-being.

The third strategy is to space out. "There is nothing I can do, so I just won't think about it." We stay busy or medicate ourselves with alcohol or just don't pay attention to how lousy we feel. We numb out. This too can have short-term benefit and can manage a short-term situation. But for long-term issues it's disastrous.

When I was a therapist, most of my clients had been using these strategies until they stopped working. Listening to their stories, it didn't surprise me that they felt messed up. What surprised me was that they weren't locked up on the back ward of a psychiatric hospital. Given what most of us have lived through as children and adults, it's amazing that we are as healthy as we are.

The human spirit is incredibly resilient. It's amazing the depth of pain and suffering we can experience and come through with our hearts and minds open, supple, and alive. But the thing that brings us down most quickly is isolation. When we aren't alone, our natural wisdom, compassion, and kindness flow even in difficult times. There is one person whose good attention we need more than anyone else's. It's the one we spend the most time with day and night: our self.

When we are busy grasping for things, being irritated with others or spacing out, we're not truly present with ourselves. We've abandoned our hurt, loneliness, fear, or grief. We've abandoned ourselves. So if we want to thrive in difficult times, it is critical to learn to be increasingly present with ourselves.

One Friday night in my apartment, I talked with my wife, Erika, and our son, Damon, on the phone. Then I thought about going to a movie, but that felt empty. I could have called someone in Sacramento, but that would not have been the same as family. I put on music that both soothed and stimulated my loneliness. I began to pace around the apartment feeling more and more frantic knowing there was no way to assuage the aching I was feeling. There was nowhere to run.

So I stopped in my living room and stood still. I realized that at that moment there were millions of people around the planet feeling as lonely as me. There were hundreds of millions grieving the deaths of loved ones. There were countless people worried about their children, concerned about making ends meet, frightened by a disease, or cowering before the threat of violence. Most of us weren't doing anything wrong. But things don't always work out in life. We all die eventually.

Our society does us a disservice in reassuring us that we are captains of our ship, directors of our fate, controllers of our future. That's nuts. We have influence, but bad things happen to good people all the time.

Standing alone in my living room I thought, "Oh, yeah. Right. This is how life is sometimes. I'm not doing anything wrong. I'm not bad for feeling bad. Stuff happens."

I stopped running from the loneliness. I sat down in a chair and just felt it. I didn't try to talk myself into or out of anything. I just stayed present. It didn't feel good. But at least I had one attentive friend in the room: me. With this, the loneliness softened. It didn't go away. But the tightness relaxed because I wasn't fighting it any more. I began to feel moist, poignant, and life-filled rather than dry and barren.

So if we want to thrive in difficult times, it's important to learn to recognize this instinctual response on its own terms. It's not a thought. It's not a concept. It's a wired-in, pre-verbal, pre-conceptual biological reflex: a mental, emotional or physical tightening. It focuses our mental faculties on finding a solution out there.

This instinct is simple and not very smart. If there's no solution, it doesn't let go. We lie awake at night worrying about our child, job, health, or relationship in an endless loop of repeating thoughts. So it's important to learn to see the inner holding directly.

As we see it fully, it tends to relax. Or we can gently invite it to soften. It's like being with a child waking up from a nightmare. We don't try to talk the child out of the bad dream. We remain present in a heartful way. We don't try to talk ourselves out of the swirl of emotions or thoughts. We just stay present.

It's very simple. But it's very difficult, because it runs counter to the instinct to focus out there. So it's important to be kind and gentle and patient with ourselves.

As we relax this inner tautness, we won't start thriving overnight. But without that tension, the spinning emotions and thoughts and feelings gradually run out of gas and begin to slow down.

With this something deeply mysterious and deeply human begins to emerge. We notice a poignant well-being that's not dependent on fixing anything. We touch a wholeness that isn't based on things we can't control.

Many people call this well-being God or the Divine or Spirit. Others call it Human Essence or Buddha nature. It makes no difference what we call it because it is pre-verbal and pre-conceptual. We just note the elusive holding, open to it in a friendly way, and relax into it.

This doesn't make us transcend the world or space out into a different realm. But it does give us the courage, heart, patience, and intelligence to come back into this world and our lives more completely, doing what is reasonable for ourselves and our fellow creatures. We stay present to what is—and with this, we are truly on a path toward thriving, even when the times are difficult.

◄○►

**DOUG KRAFT** *is a Unitarian Universalist minister, psychotherapist, and long-time student and teacher of meditation. He has trained with Buddhist teachers and dharma masters in the United States and South East Asia. His forthcoming book,* Buddha's Map, *details the elegant and powerful meditation described by the Buddha in the earliest recordings of his talks. Doug now lives in Northern California with his wife and two cats.*

# THE KNOWLEDGE ROAD
## TO NOWHERE

## MEREDITH GARMON

I grew up impressed with the need to know. And now my spiritual practice is not knowing.

My Unitarian Universalist upbringing pointed me toward the path of philosophy, but the philosophy teacher whose work compelled me most might better be described as an anti-philosopher.

My spiritual journey as a UU and a Buddhist has both illuminated and cast shadows of doubt on the claim by our tradition that religion can be a search for truth through rational exploration and debate.

I grew up impressed with the need to know, and equally impressed that many claims of knowledge were false. I was raised by two college teachers: Mom, a professor of chemistry, and Dad, a professor of English. As their first-born, I imbibed their core value: Know stuff. Dad had a plaque over his desk, quoting Plato: "There is only one good, knowledge; only one evil, ignorance."

I was raised in the South by Yankee parents who became Unitarians at about the time I was born. After a few years each in Virginia, North Carolina, and Alabama, as my parents climbed the academic ladder, we settled in Carrollton, Georgia, a small town without a Unitarian Universalist congregation. On Sundays we drove an hour to attend the UU Congregation of Atlanta.

In childhood, I had shown symptoms of the philosophy bug. I was one of those kids who, early on, was fascinated with the thought that the color experience I call "red" might be experienced by other people the way I experience blue. I was drawn to the nonsense questions—though I had no grasp on their nonsensicality. At age six, I had wanted to know, "What's the opposite of a rubber band? Which would be reversed—its elasticity or its loop shape?" The teachers at my Unitarian Universalist Sunday School classes seemed to enjoy my loopy questions—and gave me others to think about.

I was in fourth grade the first time I can remember hearing the word *atheist*. I asked what it meant and shortly thereafter decided that I was one. My Sunday School teachers did not react when I announced this to them, but my Carrollton classmates were gratifyingly scandalized. Some of them sought to rescue me from certain damnation. Naturally, I became a debater. Then a debate coach.

By my mid-twenties, I was as a graduate student in Communications Studies at Baylor University, preparing for a career as college debate coach. I took a number of classes in argumentation, where we talked a lot about justificatory devices for beliefs. I'd majored in philosophy as an undergrad and had the vague sense that some of what my philosophy professors had been carrying on about might be relevant. I had the philosophy bug. So one semester I wandered across the quad to take a course in epistemology (the theory of knowledge), in Baylor's philosophy department. The last reading assignment in the class consisted of two chapters from *Philosophy and the Mirror of Nature* by Richard Rorty.

Rorty diagnoses philosophy's obsession with knowledge, which it has had in particular since the seventeenth century, when Descartes conceived of knowledge as mirroring nature. Against this representationalist conception of knowledge, Rorty draws upon his rather freewheeling interpretations of certain other philosophers—especially John Dewey, Ludwig Wittgenstein, and Martin Heidegger—to argue for a revival of pragmatism, the American philosophy developed by Charles Peirce, William James, and Dewey in the nineteenth and early twentieth centuries. Rorty's pragmatism says that the point of inquiry is not to picture the way things really are but to cope with them. Knowing, and therefore life, isn't about mirroring or even approximately mirroring reality. Rather, it's about *doing*.

I was hooked. I read everything by Rorty I could get my hands on. I wrote my thesis on "Richard Rorty's Pragmatism: Implications for Argumentation Theory." I decided to abandon my career track and I enrolled as a PhD student at the University of Virginia, where Rorty taught. For four years I took every class he offered and pored over the pre-publication typescripts of each new essay of his as it emerged from the departmental copy machine.

I found the experience exhilarating and liberating in two ways. First, I was getting progressively clearer on the improper basis of the quest for certainty. There is no such thing as the sort of knowledge that Plato, through my father's desk plaque, had been telling me was the only good. Rorty's pragmatism absolved me of the burden to acquire such Platonic certainty. Second, not only did I not have to get that kind of knowledge, but if it's not attainable, then my evangelical grade-school classmates didn't have it either. Whew! In one fell swoop I had marked my independence from both my parents and my peers.

In due course, I met the degree requirements and joined the ranks of fresh assistant professors of philosophy. In one of my earliest lay sermons for my local Unitarian Universalist congregation, I addressed the nature of truth:

> There is no truth "out there"—just waiting, like the elephant encountered by the five blind men—for us to get our hands around more of it. Sentences are human creative products, just as art and music are. We produce beliefs—sentences to which we give our assent—as best we can to meet our purposes, and we will always be re-creating belief and knowledge as our purposes guide our inquiry and what we

learn in turn leads us to redefine our purposes. . . . Art does not aim at gradually converging toward the one ultimate eternal beauty. Nor should we see our sentences and beliefs as converging toward one ultimate eternal truth—even an infinitely far-off truth. The search for truth is not aimed at bringing itself to an end. It's not that the target is impossibly far off. It's that there is no overall target—only local and temporary targets.

For me, graduate study in philosophy was therapy, curing me of the grip of my philosophical bug. From Wittgenstein, I read that the aim of philosophy is to show the fly the way out of the fly bottle. The image stuck with me: philosophy as buzzing around inside a bottle of questions, trying to answer them, unable to see a way out.

The questions that Western philosophers regard as central have gradually shifted through the centuries, but I began to notice that the old questions weren't ever actually answered. Or, if they were, then that area of inquiry spun off into an empirical discipline and wasn't philosophy any more. Rorty notes that the history of philosophy isn't one of answering questions, but of getting over them.

One of the questions I got over, with the assistance of Wittgenstein-via-Rorty, was that color conundrum. Wittgenstein once answered the question, "How do I know it's red?" by saying, "I know it's 'red' because I speak English." In other words, "red" is a concept (for to have a concept is to be able to use a word), and all there is to do with a concept is use it in the ways appropriate to the speakers of the language within which the word or concept has its place. There's the doing—and, beyond that, there's nothing there. "Red," ultimately, is empty.

I came to Buddhism slowly. I read Hermann Hesse's *Siddhartha* in eighth grade and felt its impact like a body blow. With nowhere to go to build on that experience, it gradually faded—yet a seed had been planted. In college, I mused, captivated, over the Taoist text the *Tao Te Ching* (not strictly Buddhism, but an influence on the Zen form). As an assistant professor of philosophy at a small liberal arts school, I was called upon occasionally to teach a humanities course that included surveying world religions. As I prepared for the Buddhism unit, I found many of the teachings eerily reminiscent of what I'd spent graduate school thinking about.

In the Culamalunkya Sutta, the Buddha is presented with the sort of questions with which philosophy and religion typically wrestle: Is the world eternal or not? Finite or infinite? Is the soul the same as the body or different? Does a person exist after death or not? The Buddha replies:

> Suppose . . . a man were wounded by an arrow thickly smeared with poison, and his friends and companions, his kinsmen and relatives, brought a surgeon to treat him. The man would say, "I will not let the surgeon pull out this arrow until I know whether the man who wounded me was a noble or a Brahmin or a merchant or a worker; . . . until I know the name and clan of the man who wounded

me; . . . whether the man who wounded me was tall or short or of middle height; . . . was dark or brown or golden skinned; . . . lives in such a village or town or city; . . . until I know whether the bow that wounded me was a long bow or a crossbow; . . . the bowstring was fiber or reed or sinew or hemp or bark; . . . the shaft was wild or cultivated; . . . with what kind of feathers the shaft that wounded me was fitted; . . . with what kind of sinew the shaft that wounded me was bound; . . . whether the arrowhead [was] . . . curved or barbed or calf-toothed or lancet-shaped." All this would still not be known to that man and meanwhile he would die.

The sutra goes on to say that subscribing to any of these views—that the world is eternal, or not eternal, and so on —precludes the holy life. The Buddha refuses to address any question related to these matters because it "does not lead to disenchantment, to dispassion, to cessation, to peace, to direct knowledge, to enlightenment, to Nibbana."*

How very pragmatic! The Buddha, too, was trying to show the fly the way out of the fly bottle. What took me years more to grasp was that liberation from philosophical questions by way of a philosophical explanation of the sensicality of the questions was partial liberation at best.

---

* The Culamalunkya Sutta in *The Middle Length Discourses of the Buddha: A Translation of the Majjhima Nikaya.* Fourth Ed. (Somerville, MA: Wisdom Publications, 2009).

My call away from teaching philosophy and toward
Unitarian Universalist ministry came as a double awareness: things I can do (I'm good at public speaking; I'm
reasonably smart; I've been a UU all my life, I love our
congregations); and things I have no idea how to do (i.e.,
the *other* stuff ministers do or are, which I couldn't then
even name, skills eventually described to me as "projecting
spiritual presence"). Somehow, dimly, I perceived that the
part I was clueless about—so clueless I couldn't say what
it was—involved the next step in my journey. It was the
void I most needed to fill.

So when, after one year of seminary training for ministry,
the Midwest Regional Subcommittee on Candidacy told me
to "get a spiritual practice," I knew before I'd arrived back
home what that practice would be. I went looking for Buddhists to teach me how they practice. I spent one year with
a *vipassana* (insight) meditation teacher, and then began
checking out Zen teachers. I started sitting every day.

That was eleven years ago. I've been sitting daily and
attending retreats two to five times a year ever since.
The Rorty-*dharma* in many ways prepared me well for
the *Buddhadharma*. In Zen and Buddhism books and in
the dharma talks (*teisho*) of Zen teachers, I hear recurrent
echoes of the themes of my graduate school experience.
Attachment to your picture of reality doesn't help. *Upaya*
(skillful means) does. Concepts are empty yet useful within
a context of a particular purpose. All things are impermanent, including the list of sentences that humans, at any

given time, commend as true. Things do not have essences or permanent, distinct identities, but are continually shifting networks of relationships—and this includes the self. Rorty taught "radical contingency;" I discovered that the Buddha also taught this concept, calling it "interdependent co-origination."

However, when I first heard my Buddhist teachers talking about seeing things exactly as they are in themselves, with all our attachments and purposes dropped away, I had no idea how to charitably interpret such talk. Had not Wittgenstein established that "all seeing is seeing *as*"? There is no Kantian thing-in-itself—nor even a "red," apart from the practices and purposes of calling things red.

I don't know how to resolve this issue except in practice —that is, pragmatically. My inner Zen teacher says to me, "Never mind if everything is purposive, or not. There's a poisoned arrow that's killing you, Meredith, so let's set that question aside. Never mind about *everything* and bring mindfulness to just what is before you right now. Do you notice the presence of purpose within you? Fine. Just notice it. If, in the glare of your attention, that purposive category of perception begins to loosen its grip, does another one pop up in its stead? Fine. Just notice that one, too. Does some word or phrase arise to attach itself to your perception? Okay. Notice that, too."

We walk the path to nonlinguistic, nonpurposive *presence* one step at a time. Notice and see through the linguistic description and the purpose it serves. Then the next one, then the next, then the next. Just keep at it. This is the path.

I grew up impressed with the need to know. And now my spiritual practice is not knowing: opening myself to let each thing present itself afresh without burying it under the load of all the concepts I worked so long to acquire.

—◦—

**MEREDITH GARMON** *serves as minister at the Unitarian Universalist Fellowship of Gainesville, Florida. He also leads the Dancing Crane Zen Center and UU meditative worship services. He is a life-long Unitarian Universalist and before becoming a minister in 2004 he was an assistant professor of philosophy for four years at Fisk University.*

# DIVERGENCE AND INFLUENCE

# UU Buddhism Is Foreign to Me

### Kat Liu

**W**hen I think of Buddhism within the context of Unitarian Universalism, it is almost always with mixed feelings. On the one hand, one of the main things that drew me to Unitarian Universalism was our commitment to religious pluralism. That Unitarian Universalism recognizes multiple sources of spiritual truth is something that resonates deeply with the Chinese approach to religion in which I grew up. Historically, even if Chinese use different labels to identify themselves—Buddhist, Taoist, Confucianist— they've borrowed freely among the various traditions, embracing beliefs and practices that they find useful. So I very much want to see Buddhism expressed in our congregations, both because I want to see the religious traditions of my ancestors reflected in this faith I've chosen, and because religious diversity itself is the norm to which I'm accustomed.

On the other hand, the actual expression of Buddhism in Unitarian Universalist congregations has turned out to be complicated and occasionally painful for me. The reason, I think, is because of our Protestant roots, but not in the ways one might expect. This is not about a clash between Buddhism and Christianity but rather about the under-examined ways in which Protestant culture continues to operate in our congregations, even those who overtly reject Christianity.

Both Unitarianism and Universalism come out of the Christian Protestant tradition and so our services are on Sunday mornings, our clergy are usually called ministers, and more importantly, while the content of our sermons and songs may be different, any mainline Protestant visiting our congregations would feel comfortable with the format in which they are presented. When I first joined my Unitarian Universalist congregation, I immediately started pressuring my minister to incorporate more Eastern religious elements into Sunday worship. But getting what I wanted proved less than satisfying. I quickly learned both from my own congregation and while visiting others that we cannot take elements of Buddhist worship and overlay them onto an otherwise Protestant order of service. The result is awkward and smacks of cultural misappropriation. A Buddhist chant is not a hymn. Nor can UU ministers authentically preach about Buddhism unless they are actually familiar with it. Try to imagine a UU preacher proclaiming from the pulpit how much they "admire Christianity" and then going into a dry biography of Jesus that sounds like it was lifted from an introductory book. On the few occasions that I've seen it attempted, incorporating Buddhism into UU services made Buddhism seem even more foreign and objectified, rather than an integral to our UU faith.

There are, of course, Unitarian Universalists with a deep understanding of Buddhist tenets and practices, many much deeper than my own. But since the majority of Buddhists within Unitarian Universalism are white, middle-to-upper class liberals who took up Buddhism as adults, our views of Buddhism are very different. A great many Western Buddhists have come to Buddhism after rejecting the faith tradition in which they grew up—usually Christianity. As a result, they define Buddhism in reaction to their previous faith. I've repeatedly heard things such as, "I like Buddhism because it's atheistic (unlike Christianity)." And, "The thing I most appreciate about Buddhism is that it's based on reason, not superstitions (unlike Christianity)." When I tell them that the Buddhism with which I grew up is populated with gods—*Buddhas* and *pusas* (Mandarin for *bodhisattvas*) and other deities—and people do things that others might deem superstitious, I've often been told, sometimes with a shocking air of authority and certainty, "That isn't *real* Buddhism."

Several things go through my mind when I have these encounters. First, is my initial hurt reaction over the negation of my ancestral culture and personal experience. The proclamations I hear from these UUs ignore the numerous references to gods and miraculous events that can be found throughout even the earliest Buddhist scriptures. Even when entering into a tradition in which they were not born, some (not all) members of the white majority assume an authority that their experiences alone define what is true. Second, I have to remind myself that these people are often coming from a place of their own hurt due to negative experiences with Christianity and have found what they consider to be a refuge in Western Buddhism. They do not intend to hurt, only to defend against being hurt. Third, even with this understanding, these experiences illustrate the wide gap between how I (and maybe other Asian UUs) see Buddhism and how most white UUs see it.

The Chinese tradition in which I grew up is more inclined to absorb what is useful from other faiths than to identify itself in opposition to that which is different. (Indeed, I see the tendency for UUs to define themselves in opposition to something else as a larger issue in the denomination as a whole.) While a Chinese Buddhist would not identify as Christian, the Chinese Buddhist's identity is not focused on being "not Christian." It is focused on being Buddhist. There is no need to choose between which religion is right or which is wrong; Jesus Christ would be seen as just another of countless Buddhas. In fact, I have heard him referred to as such.

Perhaps as a result of the explicit rejection of gods and superstitions, Buddhism in Unitarian Universalist contexts, and in the U.S. in general, seems to focus almost exclusively on meditation and mindfulness. When I think of Western Buddhism, I think of meditation retreats in pleasant, quiet places. While I recognize meditation as an integral part of Buddhism—one spoke of the "dharma wheel" representing the eight-fold path—it is not the only part, and not even the key part, of the *Pure Land* and *Ch'an Buddhism* that my Chinese family practices. So the emphasis on meditation, almost to the exclusion of all else, makes Western Buddhism feel more foreign than familiar to me.

The Buddhism with which I'm familiar is a mixture of Buddhism from India, Taoism, Confucianism, and Chinese folk traditions. In Chinese temples, Buddhas, pusas, and Taoist deities all sit side by side, and the only way that you can tell the religious affiliation of the temple is by who is sitting in the "host" position. The space is buzzing at all hours and on all days as adherents stop by before or after work to make their offerings and/or ask for blessings from the appropriate deities. The air is thick with incense and chanting. Indeed, there are many ways in which Roman Catholicism feels more familiar to me than our austere UU Protestant services that are limited to Sundays and eschew all iconography and veneration. Temple tables are laden with vegetarian dishes, fruits, flowers, and other offerings. In almost every temple there is a corner where food is being collected for the needy. In Chinese homes of the more devout, there is often an altar with a statue of Amida Buddha or the bodhisattva Kwan Shih Yin, or Amida Buddha flanked by Kwan Shih Yin (Avalokitesvara) and Ta Shih

Chi (Mahasthamaprapta) (referred to here by their Chinese names, with their Sanskrit names in parentheses), toward whom daily offerings of fruits and flowers are made and chanting is directed.

Chinese Buddhism, reflecting the culture in which it arose, emphasizes relationships. The offerings that are made to ancestors and deities alike may look superstitious. And yes, there is as much graft in some Chinese Buddhist temples as there is in some Christian churches. But the act of giving—whether filling a monk's begging bowl or making offerings to the deities or donating to charity—reinforces generosity. The physical act of kowtowing to the Buddha or Kwan Shih Yin or our ancestors reinforces our humility and acknowledges that we are where we are because of those who have come before. Nuns chant not just for accumulation of their own merit but also for others. Above all, these rituals reinforce awareness of interdependency, reciprocity, and mutuality.

Moreover, the Buddhism with which I grew up seems more accessible to the average person, whereas Western Buddhism, not unlike Unitarian Universalism, seems to attract primarily relatively educated, affluent people. Even before Buddhism left India, there was already a recognition that the ideal of the *arhat* (an individual who has attained his or her own enlightenment) as laid out by the Buddha (who himself came from class and privilege) was inaccessible to the vast majority of people. Most people are too busy with familial and societal obligations to retreat into meditation. In fact, those who did were dependent upon the goodwill of householders for their meals (a dynamic that has been mostly lost in the West). So even before Buddhism left India, a new model had already begun to arise—the bodhisattva who accumulates merit on behalf of others. It was this model that caught fire in China and then spread throughout much of Asia, offering everyone— every sentient being—a way into the "Pure Land," and ultimately to *nirvana* (escape from the cycle of death and rebirth). It is a Universalist message very much in keeping with Unitarian Universalism.

I am making the case for the merits of Chinese Buddhism because I feel it is underappreciated within Unitarian Universalism, but I don't want to imply that it's "better than" Western Buddhism. I recognize that Buddhism is a proselytizing religion. I also know that the word *proselytizing* makes many UUs uncomfortable. By proselytizing I do not mean that Buddhist nuns will knock on your door asking whether you've attained enlightenment, nor that you'll see Buddhists insisting that you must convert lest you burn in Buddhist hell. I mean that Buddhism is inherently open to accepting converts who come from different cultures. The majority of religions in this world—including Judaism, Hinduism, and all of the indigenous traditions—are meant for people born into their respective communities and are thus tied to ethnicity. It's not that you can't convert (and be fully welcome), but those religions are not geared toward such, and converts are generally thought of as having joined the "tribe" (think of the Jewish ritual of circumcision). In contrast, Christianity, Islam, Buddhism, and a few others are open to people joining from outside the culture in which those religions originated. As a result, those religions have adapted to fit their new local cultures. So just as Chinese Buddhists interpreted the *dharma* through the influences of Taoism and other indigenous traditions, so too Western Buddhists (who are primarily educated, affluent, and atheistic) have adapted the dharma for their culture. Both Chinese Buddhism and Western Buddhism believe in the four noble truths, the three marks of existence, and the eight-fold path and thus both are authentically Buddhist.

There are a variety of ways in which I, as an Asian American, agree more with the Western Buddhist community than with Chinese Buddhists. For one thing, Western Buddhists tend to affirm equality for women; for lesbian, gay, bisexual, and transgender folks; and for others who are often treated as "less than" in traditional Asian society. Along that vein, the concept of social justice and working for it in this lifetime is much more fully developed in the West.

I do not argue better or worse between these types of Buddhism but instead bring up for discussion some of the issues that arise when UUs adopt Buddhism as a practice. Ultimately, I hope that we draw from the best of what both Chinese and Western Buddhism have to offer and bring that to Unitarian Universalism. Creativity and vibrancy emerge out of the interactions between differences. The creative flourishing of the Unitarian Transcendentalists was largely due to the influence of Hindu and Buddhist teachings. Within Unitarian Universalism, I see the potential for a great synthesis of Buddhist and other dharmic faiths, our Jewish and Christian roots, and the important influences of humanism and Earth-based and indigenous traditions.

◄○►

**KAT LIU** *grew up with Chinese Buddhist/folk traditions at home and exposure to Christianity at school and in the larger society. She holds a doctorate in biology from Caltech and worked for several years as a neurobiologist before changing paths to study religious studies at Georgetown. She has worked for the UUA's Multicultural Growth and Witness staff group for six years and is the 2012–2013 Fahs Fellow for Innovation in Spiritual Practices.*

# Diversity Within Buddhism

## Jeff Wilson

"**N**am Myoho Renge Kyo! Nam Myoho Renge Kyo! Yo Yo Yo!" rapped four white boys from Connecticut as I sat under my umbrella in New York City's Union Square, surrounded on all sides by gray skyscrapers and madly rushing taxi cabs. The crowd of about a thousand—including Caucasians, Latinos, and Asians, but at least 50 percent African-American—enthusiastically rapped the mantra back at them, shaking and boogieing before the stage. I scribbled a few notes in my pad and tapped my foot to the beat. It was just another day in the diverse world of New York City Buddhism.

A lot of Unitarian Universalists interested in Buddhism live in areas where they have little or no contact with other Buddhists or with trained *dharma* teachers. I had the opposite problem: When I lived in New York City from 1997 to 2001, I had so much Buddhism at my fingertips that it took me months to do the research necessary for my book,

*The Buddhist Guide to New York.* The Buddhism of New York City, experienced in all its diversity, is about as fascinating as you could imagine.

Take the Soka Gakkai folks, who were putting on the rainy festival I attended. This community's commitment to racial inclusivity puts our UU congregations to shame. They perform same-sex marriages, spend significant amounts of time and money on social justice, and don't shave their heads or perform strict austerities to become holy. They, too, respect the inherent worth of all people, recognize the interdependent web of all things, and believe in a direct, personal quest for meaning. They also think that repeatedly chanting their mantra can help you acquire a new car or job and that the holy power of the universe is contained in a scroll penned by a Japanese priest who died seven hundred years ago.

Then there's the apartment downtown where college professors sit facing the wall and try to achieve sudden enlightenment while a Zen master performs elaborately stylized rituals in the middle of the room. Or the loft in midtown where a Socratic discussion in the finest classical Greek style is being held: The participants are energetically debating an ancient Indian how-to manual for aspiring Buddhas, moderated by an American Buddhist monk who sells high-fashion accessories based on his robes and a wizened Tibetan man who claims be a reincarnated saint. Or the Buddhist church uptown, where parishioners sing hymns with organ accompaniment, pass the collection plate, and listen quietly to a Sunday-morning sermon from the minister while paying their respects to the Amida Buddha, whose universal grace ensures them rebirth in the Western Paradise of Pure Bliss.

With so much diversity, one begins to wonder what is the common thread that holds all these different ideas and practices together as "Buddhism." And the more Buddhism(s) one rubs up against, the more it becomes apparent that the little nibble UUs are taking encompasses only a small percentage of the religion as a whole.

One of the most interesting things to me about my explorations in the chaotic subculture of New York City Buddhism is not only how elements of Buddhism coincide with Unitarian Universalist values and styles but also how other elements conflict with those values and styles. For instance, take the UU Principle of the inherent worth and dignity of all people and compare it to the Buddhist idea of inherent Buddha nature. There are some obvious similarities between these two sentiments, and they help to flesh each other out. The UU Principle seems to make a statement *a priori* about the worth of human beings, without explaining why we should be regarded as valuable and dignified. Applying the idea of Buddha nature, we can say that this inherent goodness comes from the potential of every person to become a compassionate, wise, helpful human being who works to alleviate the suffering of other people. And because Buddha nature resides in all sentient beings, the UU statement can be stretched further to become more encompassing: We affirm and promote the inherent worth and dignity of all living things.

On the other hand, there are elements of Buddhism that at first seem to directly contradict the UU approach to religion. We often like to think of Buddhism as a rational, nontheistic method for people to seek their own mental freedom. For many, our Buddhist ideal might be an enlightened Zen master who disdains prayer, scriptures, and ritual. He just meditates, achieves a breakthrough, and doesn't fuss with all the trappings of religion that UUs often seem to scorn. But that's a fantasy conjured up to satisfy our own longings, one that doesn't resemble how people in Asia have practiced and understood the dharma for the past twenty-five hundred years. During my New York City Buddhist explorations, I received holy water blessings from Theravada monks who tied sacred strings around my wrist; learned about Chinatown believers who generate merit by releasing thousands of turtles into Central Park every year; and had my fortune told for a dollar at a temple. One Japanese group I met with believes that misfortune in one's life is caused by the lingering bad *karma* and evil spirits left over from the past, and advocates purification rituals and exorcisms as the most expedient religious practices.

Perhaps the most extreme example of this apparent irrationality is Pure Land Buddhism, which is the largest, most widespread form of Buddhism practiced today. Everywhere I went, from Japanese to Chinese to Korean to Tibetan to Vietnamese temples, I encountered people praying before images of Amitabha Buddha, the Buddha of Infinite Light and Life. The people at the New York Buddhist Church told me that enlightenment cannot be achieved by one's own efforts—it comes solely as a gift from the "Other Power." Doesn't this go against everything we've been taught as self-reliant, self-confidently agnostic Unitarian Universalists?

In struggling with this seemingly contradictory Buddhist teaching, however, I came to realize how familiar it really was. Our denomination is formed out of the marriage of two great, courageous faith traditions: the Unitarians and the Universalists. And the more I practiced and examined Pure Land Buddhism, the more I realized that it was remarkably similar to the good news our Universalist forefathers and mothers spread throughout the land. The Pure Landers say not to worry about having a bad rebirth, because the nature of the universe is inherently compassionate and will shepherd you to happiness and wisdom. Spiritual attainment comes through humility, thankfulness, and the desire to bring joy to others, not from subtly ego-driven quests for purity, holiness, and self-generated wisdom. As I came to appreciate and respect the deep modesty, sincerity, and generosity of the Pure Land Buddhists I chanted with, I realized that these same values had been passed on to me through the historically Universalist church in which I grew up. A desire arose in me to go back and understand my own theological ancestors and their wisdom more deeply. The Buddhists who had at first seemed the most different from me, in the end gave me back a crucial part of my past that I'd forgotten I'd left behind.

There are limits to how much one can learn from the truly odd, of course. I didn't take away much of value from the New Jersey group that claims their leader is the Buddha and that has communed with intelligent vegetable life on the planet Venus.

Some of the differences that may seem strange to Western UUs are just cultural aspects, of course. I remember sitting on an orange children's stool at a *vihara* (Buddhist monestary) in residential Queens, my knees up around my ears as I talked with Sri Lankan monks lounging on sofas. Monks command great respect in their tradition, and in their culture one never sits or stands so that one's head is higher than their superior's. This was a challenge when I had to chaperone a five-foot monk with the hip-hop sounding nickname Bhante G around the city—but let's not pretend that we UUs don't have our own similarly culture-bound rituals and traditions. I never found any equivalent to my church's Committee on Committees at the *sanghas* I visited, or came across people whose true worship service was Coffee Hour and whose holy water was java.

Perhaps the best lesson to be learned from all this Buddhist exploration was how wisdom comes packaged in so many different forms. The Lotus Sutra teaches about *upaya*, the idea that different people need different methods and symbols in order to understand the universe, and that all sincere spiritual pilgrims will reach the summit regardless of their path. It's a deep truth that we explicitly affirm in our own UU Sources, wherein we call attention to the value of Jewish, Christian, humanist, Pagan, and mystic insights, as well as the wisdom of all the prophets who have shone light on what it takes to live a meaningful human life. Certainly my UU upbringing gave me the tools to navigate this diverse world of Buddhist groups in a respectful, open-minded way. And I found personal benefit from all the different methods of chanting, meditating, visualizing, and thinking that I learned.

It's hard to predict what Unitarian Universalist Buddhism will look like someday. But it might resemble something like the dharma the Won Buddhists practice in their little gray temple by the Queensboro Bridge. Their leadership is nearly 70 percent female, just as more than 50 percent of our own clergy are women. The Won Buddhists are fundamentally oriented toward applying Buddhist teachings to everyday life in the real world and believe that spiritual progress should match ever-increasing material progress. They avoid elaborate rituals and systems of symbolism, worshipping before the simple image of a perfect black circle on a white background, representing the pure, naturally whole nature of the universe. Instead of golden Buddha statues, they focus on recognizing the Buddhas within the everyday people they meet on the street. They teach that the scriptures must be understood in light of modern knowledge and science, while maintaining moderate devotional chanting that helps open the heart and develop compassion and gratitude. Lay people elect a Board of Directors for each Won temple and have significant governing power over the group's activities and finances. Their sense of compassion and interconnectedness drives them to agitate for world peace at the United Nations and perform community service in their neighborhood. And interestingly, they keep personal journals of their spiritual activities throughout the day, checking off when they perform the minimum number of charitable deeds and traditional practices advocated by their ministers.

Whatever may lie in our futures, I know I had a fun and thought-provoking experience as a Unitarian Universalist getting to know more about the myriad ways in which people approach the dharma. Even the the diminutive Chinese nun who runs a vegetarian restaurant that doubles as a temple dedicated to a gigantic War bodhisattva held hidden teachings. And of course for everything I encountered that struck me as strange, I found three things that made me grateful for my opportunities to explore Buddhism in depth. In the end, the really gratifying thing was finding that Buddhism helped me to be a better UU, and being a UU helped me to be a better Buddhist.

# An Egoless Dance for Our Congregational Life

## Thandeka

**W**hen I met Gunapala Dharmasiri in 1994, he shook my hand as if we were reunited old friends. I was an assistant professor at Williams College in Massachusetts and he, a Theravada Buddhist ethicist, scholar, and author of *Fundamentals of Buddhist Ethics*, was on campus to deliver a public lecture. Dharmasiri, as I quickly learned, had read my review of his book in *The Pacific World: Journal of the Institute of Buddhist Studies*—and he liked what he read.

"Ah, Thandeka," he said, "You understood my book better than any other reviewer in the United States."

I was pleased by his comment, but not surprised. My own Unitarian Universalist religious experiences, combined with my personal practice of *vipassana* or insight meditation, gave me the perspective I needed to understand, explain, and affirm his delineation of the two forms of

Buddhist morality that he calls ordinary morality and en-lightenment morality. These same personal experiences, however, also showed me why Unitarian Universalists must reach beyond our personal Buddhist practices in order to revitalize our religious communities.

I thus felt gratitude to meet the man whose work I so deeply admired. And I felt joy that we could meet so wholeheartedly as two persons from two different religious traditions. More precisely, even though I practice medita-tion techniques from his Buddhist tradition, I do so always as a Unitarian Universalist rather than as a Buddhist, be-cause my religious community is not a Buddhist *sangha*; it's a Unitarian Universalist congregation.

Many of us engage in Buddhist practices as Unitarian Universalists in order to achieve an egoless, spontaneous morality. We meditate, and often feel transformed by our practice, if only fleetingly. And we continue our practice in order to extend our ability to act selflessly, morally, and compassionately.

So we are not particularly interested in what Dharmasiri calls ordinary morality. Ordinary morality is akin to what Westerners like to think of as the Golden Rule. The ratio-nale for this kind of moral behavior is self-interest. I won't do harm to others, the reasoning goes, so others won't harm me. Dharmasiri rightly calls this kind of morality "calcu-lated." Unitarian Universalists tend to aspire to practice the other form of Buddhist morality, described by Dharmasiri as egoless morality.

Egoless Buddhist morality is spontaneous rather than calculated. Enlightened persons practice this kind of morality, says Dharmasiri, and have moved beyond Golden Rule moral values without abrogating them. Such persons, in Buddhist terms, are not conditioned by morality (*silamayo*) but instead are moral by nature (*silava*) because they have attained *nirvana*, which is moral perfection. When these persons perform an action, "only the action is there (*kiriya-matta*)." These persons, in Western terms, are not motivated by an expectation of an end result (i.e., a teleological ethic). Nor do they perform their actions as a kind of Kantian duty for its own sake (i.e., a deontological ethic). Rather, the enlightened person is a Buddha, someone who need not and does not *practice* charity because charity is itself the person's nature. Moral actions thus flow forth from an egoless state, as spontaneous happenings. Egoless Buddhist morality is a way of life born from a practice of right action, right mindfulness, right speech, right livelihood, and so much more.

We Unitarian Universalists embrace Buddhist practices to become an enlightened, non-anxious compassionate presence in the world.

Our individual personal Buddhist practices, however, are neither designed nor intended to replace our collective experiences in our Sunday morning services. On Sunday mornings, we sing together, listen to music and the spoken word, share our joys and concerns, participate in the offertory, attend to announcements, and then go to the coffee hour. These collective experiences, quite frequently, do not create collective experiences of individual egoless transformation. So we go home and meditate—for the most part, alone.

Our Buddhist practices, in short, do not alter our congregational lives. They amend them. This strategy, however, makes us witnesses to our own congregational demise. Here's why.

The individual members of our Unitarian Universalist congregations collectively make up the second wealthiest religious group in the United States. Our members are also the most highly educated. Almost 50 percent of us are college graduates and our average annual household income is $51,206. This is not the financial profile of the power elite. It's the profile of civil servants, schoolteachers, small businesspersons, and middle managers. In effect, Unitarian Universalist congregations are middle America— the group of professionals who keep America running by training its children, maintaining government, operating small businesses, and paying taxes. Nevertheless, Unitarian Universalists are at the absolute bottom when it comes to the amount of money we give to support our congregations. At best, we maintain our present status as small congregations because only two out of the seven persons who visit our congregations return and nine out of ten of our youth do not join UU congregations when they grow up. Our work to maintain a liberal congregation is thus a constant struggle for so many of our ministers and lay leaders because our congregational resources are always on the brink of depletion.

Two rules of thumb help explain these congregational facts of our lives: financial apathy and spiritual disengagement. We spend money on what moves us, what pleases us, and what helps us to survive and thrive. We, in short, spend our money on what is worthwhile to us. The collective lack of attention to our home congregations indicates our collective financial indifference.

Congregations cannot grow in size if their congregants are spiritually disenchanted. Disenchanted congregants do not create spiritual energy. Spiritual energy is created when—as UU minister Gordon McKeeman has reminded us—all that we do together is ministry. But so often, when we gather together in our Sunday morning services, our interests and concerns are scattered rather than united because our worship services do not cohere as an orchestration of music and words, feelings and thoughts, that create within us and among us a collective sense of unity as one faith community with many diverse voices. We ought to be filled to overflowing by a grace created within each of us by all of us ministering together so that when we are alone we can still gain strength from our religious life together—our congregation-generated spiritual heat has become the fire in our bones. But if there isn't enough spiritual energy—enough heat—generated by the congregation, visitors pose a threat to the congregation's scarcest resource: spiritual energy to revitalize de-energized, bone-cold souls. Visitors, in short, want access to this precious heat. So they are shunted aside.

Our personal Buddhists practices do not address these two major problems in our congregational life. They can't do so because these problems are religious community problems; they require Unitarian Universalist community strategies rather than personal individual Buddhist practices. Our Buddhist practices, in sum, do not help us to *feel* and *spontaneously practice* our faith collectively as an egoless communal dance. Consider the following example.

Several years ago, I met with a Catholic priest who had spent several months in Ethiopia doing famine relief work with people from a local village. The priest was a tall middle-aged man whose body weight and size seemed more suited for the heavy gear of a football lineman than the willowy garments worn by a man of the cloth.

I was then still a television producer at NBC in Los Angeles and had arranged an interview with the priest as background work for a program I wanted to produce on religious missions.

During the course of the interview, he described a personal experience in Ethiopia that had changed his life. He had participated in a dance in which the members of the devastated community spent countless hours rhythmically moving in a circle to the beat of a single drum.

Without food to forage or land to cultivate, the members of the village could do nothing except wait for their next shipment of food to be flown in. But instead of simply waiting, they danced a slow step that consisted of something that by the account of the priest seemed to consist of a "one-two-three-jump" sequence. The villagers did this for hours on end.

Wanting to be accepted as a full member of the group, the priest joined in, which immediately brought him face to face with a seemingly insurmountable problem: He was dance impaired. He could never jump at the right time. He jumped too soon or too late, or sometimes he simply forgot to jump at all. Needless to say, these missteps provided the rest of the members of the group with countless hours of laughter.

The children, quite frequently, were so amused that they would fall out of the circle, onto the ground in fits of giggling delight. All of the humor, however, was good natured. The priest said it was neither intended nor experienced as ridicule. Instead, it felt more like the bemused jesting that goes on in a community when someone marches to the beat of a different drummer.

Hour after hour, the priest labored to learn to count and then jump in just the right way. How many times did he move in and then out of step with the group's rhythm? Too many to count, he confessed, but as time wore on, something happened that took him completely by surprise.

Tears now welled in the priest's eyes and he was silent for a long moment. When he finally spoke, his voice seemed no louder than a whisper and I had to move closer in order to hear his words. "You know," he said, "until that experience

I thought that I had known God all of my life. But only as I danced with the other members of the group did I actually *feel* God's presence in my life."

The priest felt unconditional love, love beyond belief. He felt, in his theistic terms, God's love. In nontheistic terms, he felt a love so abundant and full that the experience pushed him beyond his own thoughts about God into the midst of an enormous love that changed and transformed his heart. So he danced not because he calculated it to be what he should do to fit into the community, but he danced spontaneously because his very nature danced. He danced egolessly with his dancing community.

Most of our congregations do not create literal or figurative egoless dances. We can't move freely and spontaneously as moral agents because we are, in the words of Ralph Waldo Emerson, "corpse-cold." Emerson made this diagnosis almost two centuries ago and urged clergy to preach "life passed through the fire of thought." Ministers must become holy bards, he insisted, with firsthand experiences of God. But Emerson did not teach liberal clergy and laity how to do this kind of liberal heart work. Instead, Emerson abandoned his own Unitarian ministry and left his congregation. The stakes are too high for us to walk away today. Liberal mainstream congregations—the spiritual center of American democracy—are, to quote politician Rick Santorum, "in shambles."

We risk abandoning our congregations today, however, when our personal Buddhist practices warm our individual hearts but leave the hearth of our congregational life cold. Our collective spirit needs heat that flows from the liturgical coordination of music and the spoken word in our Sunday services. Neither tambourines nor drums are required for this collective practice. Nor do we need any of the other kinds of "evangelical shows" that so many Unitarian Universalists temperamentally dislike. We do not even have to dance in the aisles. Rather, we simply have to pay attention to a three-fold process entailed in our Sunday services.

- *The individual's personal experience of a change of heart*: Congregants should feel better by the end of the service than they felt before the service began so that they have new energy to handle the struggles, difficulties, trials, and triumphs in their lives with wholehearted spiritual integrity.

- *The congregation's liturgical template*: An ethos of care and compassion should be created liturgically within the sanctuary through music, song, and other practices that support and encourage uplifting experiences of a change of heart within the gathered community.

- *The spoken word*: Sermons and homilies should narrate, support, explain, and affirm how and why the personal experience of a change of heart takes place within the present congregation.

Skillful attention to these three elements by ministers and lay leaders come to the fore when there is a coordinated theological and liturgical focus on what we feel, say, and do in our Sunday services. We must link the ministries of music and words through weekly production meetings that strengthen the ability of ministers and lay leadership to understand how music, words, and emotions can be linked together to increase the narrative flow of the Sunday sermons and other narrative structures. We must enhance liturgical styles that support and encourage good steward-ship and we must design new participatory strategies and age-appropriate liturgical and theological practices that liturgically delight and transform children.

These kinds of liturgical strategies, which focus on emboldening our faith experiences in our Sunday services, will create new personal and congregational experiences of love beyond belief, because we are a religious people who strive to stand on the side of love, who love persons rather than creeds, who affirm love as the doctrine of our church, and who practice love as a motive force for our faith-based social justice work in the world. By enhancing our ability to collectively love beyond belief through our Sunday morning worship services, we generate the spiritual energy that sustains us—love.

These kinds of congregational strategies of ministering together are not Buddhist; they are Unitarian Universalist. And they work for us because we are not a *sangha,* a Bud-dhist community; we are practicing Unitarian Universalist congregations, churches, fellowships, and societies that need help in fine-tuning our liturgical practices.

And thus my final point. Those of us who have personal Buddhist practices should strive evermore to enhance our own Unitarian Universalist faith rather than to replace it. And we should also strive to enhance our congregational life through new, collective Unitarian Universalist liturgical strategies for our Sunday services. When we do both together, we dance.

―◦―

**THANDEKA** *is a Unitarian Universalist minister, theologian, journalist, Emmy award-winning television producer, and congregational consultant and organizer. Creator of the "We Love Beyond Belief" project for congregations, she was given the !Xhosa name Thandeka, which means "beloved," by Archbishop Desmond Tutu in 1984. She has written numerous books and articles and has taught at Harvard Divinity School, Brandeis University, Williams College, and Meadville Lombard Theological School, among other institutions.*

# CONFESSIONS OF A ZEN TEACHER
# AND UU MINISTER

## JAMES ISHMAEL FORD

One of the classic markers of Unitarian Universalism is freedom, and this freedom is generally understood as self-direction, hence the old joke, "I don't belong to an organized religion. I'm a UU." Unitarian Universalism has a deep confidence that we, each of us, have all it takes within us as human beings to find purpose and direction in our lives. Zen Buddhism agrees with this but also offers a specific route to finding that freedom while avoiding the false guides of our appetite or aversion. The route is a specific path, a tradition, a teaching system. And as a teaching system it is hierarchical—necessarily so. Among the principal distinctions between these two traditions, Unitarian Universalist religious organizations, following that guiding star of maximum personal self-direction, are ultimately much flatter than a Zen group can ever be.

This distinction can be confusing to some people, as many see Zen as spontaneity itself, or even as some form of zoning out from the hubbub of life, dancing deeply into non sequitur, such as we get in the *The Daily Show*'s "moment of Zen." To further confuse things, Zen is, indeed, about freedom. But the "moment of Zen" and spontaneity are funhouse-mirror understandings of Zen's freedom—Zen's enlightenment—which is something intimately connected to a disciplined spiritual path.

This confusion comes honestly enough. There is a pretty widespread, if romantic, view that disassociates Zen's awakening from Zen's training. This romantic view of Zen was first presented in the West by the scholar-practitioner D. T. Suzuki and widely spread by his acolyte, Alan Watts. Since then, a host of writers, including many on the Internet today, have followed—all pointing to the freedom to be found at the heart of Zen, without much reference—frequently in fact, no reference—to it as a specific spiritual discipline. And here's the complication: There is truth in this. Zen is about awakening. Zen is all about awakening, awakening to who we are, and it is a way of genuine freedom.

However, Zen is at the same time very much a specific discipline or, more properly, a small basket of disciplines transmitted from teacher to disciple, helping people to find that awakening, that freedom at the heart of life and death properly encountered. This is important. That last part—"teacher to disciple"—is, on the face of it, hierarchical.

This doesn't mean that an authentic Zen cannot flatten the shape of the teacher-student relationship vastly more than the way it has come to us from Japan and Korea and Vietnam and China. In fact, as Zen makes its way from East Asia to America and the West in order to become a Western spiritual practice I believe it *must* flatten that teacher-student relationship. And I think it can. More importantly, it can do this without damaging the rich possibilities of the Zen path.

This is all a long way around the barn to speak of Boundless Way Zen. While Boundless Way is not the only experiment in that flattening, it is doing it consciously and uniquely, doing it informed by a successful and particularly flat religious community—Unitarian Universalism.

Boundless Way is a network of about ten Zen communities bound together by a shared commitment to a style of practice; a clear ethical code; a commitment to transparency, particularly regarding the ways of training; and most of all by a council of teachers who work closely and collaboratively, supporting each other and holding each other accountable. Boundless Way Zen is growing pretty rapidly. Our administrative center is in Worcester, Massachusetts, and the majority of our sitting groups are still in New England, although we are, at this writing, conducting a dialogue to bring another network of Zen *sanghas* in Ohio into our collective.

Another particularly distinctive feature of Boundless Way is that we are a hybrid lineage, combining the Soto/Harada Yasutani lineage derived from Japan and the Seung Sahn lineage derived from Korea. We appear to be the first Zen community attempting to bring such a range of lineages together.

Our training includes the discipline of *shikantaza* (just sitting), and constellated practices, as well as *koan* introspection. All our authorized teachers are eligible to join the American Zen Teachers Association, a supportive gathering of Zen teachers organized in North America. Boundless Way also transmits the Japanese Soto Zen priest ordination, registering our priests with the Soto Zen Buddhist Association, a North American proto-denominational structure still in formation but which includes the majority of people ordained in that tradition. In addition to providing spiritual direction for Zen practitioners, Boundless Way offers group practice periods on a weekly or more frequent meditation schedule; we also schedule regular retreats, from a half-day to seven days in length.

For the first decade of its existence Boundless Way was led by three transmitted teachers who, while standing in the lineage system of Zen, also have longtime connections to the UU world, as congregants, as leaders of the churches they've joined, and, in my case, as ordained UU ministers. A fourth teacher has since joined us and, while not a UU, has attended UU churches from time to time, is knowledgeable about the culture, and is committed to the larger goals inspired by the Unitarian Universalist Association.

Unitarian Universalist congregations have long seen that ministerial leadership is complex. It includes a variety of skill sets, ranging from preaching to teaching to facilitating meetings to reading a balance sheet and talking frankly about what it takes to make the institution go. The list is much longer, but this is a good beginning. UUs have also learned that a minister is not going to have all these skills. The wise search committee looks for someone who is good in two or maybe three areas, and everyone understands that the leadership of the church is ultimately distributive, with lay participation critical. Boundless Way has benefitted from this wisdom.

We've seen how important the teachers are in setting the goals and vision of this organization in ways not directly consonant with Unitarian Universalist ideals. A clash of traditional ways of handling authority took place in one situation where the teachers felt it was time to act in the purchase of a property, while the Board was not unanimously behind the move. This painfully revealed that the teachers had more final say than anyone had felt comfortable acknowledging. This left a number of people, including teachers, feeling wounded, a stage in our growth that haunts me personally.

We took away two key learnings from this situation. First, we needed to recommit to transparency. And within that transparency, to more frankly acknowledge, both for the teachers and for the community, that we are not simply a Zen UU church. Second, while there may be circumstances when a teacher's view on a specific matter will prevail, that doesn't mean we shouldn't try hard to acknowledge all the participants as having authentic stakes in the matter. And as we grow and more teachers are trained and recognized or join us, the Board's role and independence are expected to grow.

No doubt this is all influenced by our Unitarian Universalist connections. But personally, Unitarian Universalism has influenced me more as a Zen teacher than as a person.

I started with Zen. I'd been a monastic for a couple of years, and, frankly, had fallen into a group that was severely authoritarian, even cultish. When I left that group I thought I was well done with the whole thing. But the practices and the hints of insight that I'd experienced haunted me. And after some years wandering about exploring other options, I resumed my practice. At the same time I'd begun attending Unitarian Universalist worship services. And by the time I committed to training with a new Zen teacher I'd already formally signed the book at a UU congregation.

Over the next decades my spiritual life was cross-informed by the deep importance of both traditions. Mostly, I believe, to the good. But the most important time for these connections and their different foci was when I became a Zen teacher. I'd already been serving as a UU minister for nearly a decade when I was given permission to give interviews and to guide people; I'd been serving for fifteen years when I was given final authorization as an independent Zen teacher through the Rinzai-Zen *Inka Shomei* ceremony.

In the West, a Zen teacher traditionally conducts dharma transmission as an independent leader of an autonomous group. The accountability in this process is hit or miss. More recently, those in the Japanese Soto lineages have attempted to gather these teachers into a proto-denominational structure —the Soto Zen Buddhist Association. I am a member of this organization, as are all other Boundless Way priests. Even so, the bonds of authority are tenuous and entirely voluntary. The other grouping of Zen teachers, the American Zen Teachers Association, which all Boundless Way transmitted teachers also belong to, is strictly a gathering for mutual support, and the majority of members resist any suggestions of being more than that. So, for all practical purposes typical Zen teachers are from that point on, on their own.

I, however, was serving as a minister as well—not the same thing by a long shot, but it is spiritual leadership, and it has a lot of accountability. I was surrounded by people who either didn't particularly care that I was a spiritual leader, or had authority issues that I had to deal with. Not always fun, but always useful.

It reminds me of two old Zen sayings. The first is that the Buddha is still training. And the second saying, deeply related to the first, is that the Way is one continuous mistake. This sense was very much in the air when Melissa Blacker and David Rynick and I came together as the founding teachers of Boundless Way.

My UU ministry has taught me a great deal about how to be with people at once with some leadership and as just one of the gang. This has shaped who I am as a Zen teacher as well as who I am as a person.

But as a Zen teacher, probably the most important thing that comes out of my Unitarian Universalist life is how I'm constantly pushed into action. Now, I think a real shadow for UUs is action without a spiritual context. I'm unmoved by the notion that social justice is my religion. This view lacks grounding, and I've seen the impulse go awry in any number of ways.

But a genuine interior life, a real spiritual practice, needs to be manifested. Zen Buddhists, in my experience, tend to minimize that manifestation in the world.

A Japanese proverb summarizes all this succinctly: "Vision without action is a dream, while action without vision is a nightmare." My Unitarian Universalist proclivity to be engaged meets my Zen Buddhist practices and perspectives that ground what those actions might best look like. Out of that meeting, I find a whole life. Or pretty darned close.

This dual inclination has seeped into who I am as a Zen teacher. How are our lives manifesting into actions from the perspectives found deep within the practices and perspectives of Zen? This is a drum I continue to beat.

And that beat resonates in these difficult times and among troubled hearts. So I find myself deeply grateful for both the traditions that have nurtured and inspired my life.

Today I can no longer say Unitarian Universalist *or* Zen Buddhist. There simply isn't enough separation to make the distinction.

One thing.
And for this I am endlessly grateful.

—◦—

**JAMES ISHMAEL FORD, ROSHI** *is senior minister of the First Unitarian Church of Providence, Rhode Island. He is also the founding abbot of the Boundless Way Zen network and serves as a senior guiding teacher there. He has written widely on Zen Buddhism, Unitarian Universalism, spirituality, and social engagement. His most recent book is* If You're Lucky, Your Heart Will Break: Field Notes from a Zen Life, *from Wisdom Publications.*

# AFTERWORD

## WAYNE ARNASON AND SAM TRUMBORE

At the conclusion of a Zen *sesshin* (extended meditation retreat) it is usual to have brief liturgy in which all the instruments that have helped the students mark the time during chanting and sitting are sounded one last time in a closing sequence of sounds. Each instrument is heard in its uniqueness. There is no effort to blend them all into one or to play a composition that uses all the instruments. The liturgy, which includes words from the liturgical leader of the sesshin, begins: "Let me respectfully remind you, life and death are of supreme importance. We must strive to awaken, awaken."

These closing reflections represent something similar for this book. In bringing these Unitarian Universalist Buddhist practitioners' voices together into one volume, we offer a snapshot rather than a comprehensive analysis of the relationship between Buddhism and Unitarian Universalism. There was much that we did not explore or include in the collection. There are voices from UU Buddhists we wish we could have included. In his "A Brief History" essay Jeff Wilson acknowledges the relationship between the Japanese lay Buddhist movement Rissho Kosei-Kai and Unitarian Universalism. Rissho Kosei-Kai plays a significant role in Buddhism in Japan and in the world's interfaith efforts. Relationships with Rissho Kosei-Kai leaders have influenced Unitarian Universalist leaders in ways that have yet to be documented. We regret that we were unable to explore this relationship more deeply in this volume.

One of the questions we leave unanswered is whether Buddhism's influence in Unitarian Universalism will continue to be exerted through individuals or through any ongoing organized presence. Local sitting groups meeting in Unitarian Universalist congregations and publicized through church media do make a difference in who is attracted to UU congregations. However, as Thandeka points out in her essay, the personal spiritual practice disciplines and depth that UU Buddhist groups encourage may not be what Unitarian Universalism most needs to survive, thrive, and grow in the century ahead. At the denominational level, ongoing doubt remains about how much individual UU Buddhists want to gather for regular study and practice in biennial conferences. Most practitioners focus on their local affiliations, and those who care to do the institutional work for maintaining Buddhist *sanghas* prioritize local UU sanghas or their Buddhist lineage communities. Locally focused sanghas with different lineages and practices may find more affinity within their tradition rather than in the occasional convocations and workshops of the UU Buddhist Fellowship.

Currently the UUA is exploring gatherings of Unitarian Universalists beyond the congregational setting. One such gathering may be a strong eclectic Buddhist sangha that chooses to affiliate with the UUA. Another possibility might be a UU minister with a committed Buddhist practice who seeks to form a congregation with meditation and dharma talks at the core of the Sunday morning service. A number of sitting groups associated with the Insight Meditation Society in Massachusetts and with Spirit Rock Meditation Center in California have much affinity and overlapping membership with Unitarian Universalism. We expect to see institutional experimentation arising from the contemporary wave of enthusiasm for Buddhism in the West.

This enthusiasm is evident in the lively exploration of Buddhist literature and media about what "liberal Buddhism" means in the West. Unitarian Universalists who practice Buddhism are an important part of that exploration. Western Buddhism continues to evolve. A small number of monastic communities and temples are well established, but the increasing number of Buddhist practitioners is taking place in more lay-led, secularized, and informal settings.

Unitarian Universalist polity offers Buddhists of various schools some insight into what is possible when you seek to build a nonhierarchical democratic religious community that invites authentic spiritual depth and practice. We look to a future in which Unitarian Universalism and Buddhism are mutually interdependent and co-arising, changing each other and changing the world.

So without knowing where this future will take us, we can only hold before us as counsel and challenge the words that close each Zen sesshin: "Take heed—do not squander your life!"

# FOR FURTHER READING

Aitken, Robert. *Taking the Path of Zen.* New York: Farrar, Strauss and Giroux, 1982.

Amero, Bhikkhu. *Small Boat, Great Mountain: Theravadan Reflections on The Natural Great Perfection.* Redwood Valley, CA: Abhayagiri Monastic Foundation, 2003.

Batchelor, Stephen. *Buddhism Without Beliefs: A Contemporary Guide to Awakening.* New York: Riverhead Books, 1998.

Beck, Charlotte J. and Steve Smith. *Nothing Special: Living Zen.* New York: HarperCollins, 1993.

Brach, Tara. *Radical Acceptance: Embracing Your Life with the Heart of a Buddha.* New York: Bantam, 2004.

Brantley, Jeffrey. *Calming Your Anxious Mind: How Mindfulness and Compassion Can Free You from Anxiety, Fear and Panic.* Oakland, CA: New Harbinger Publications, 2007.

Buswell, Robert E., Jr. *Tracing Back the Radiance: Chinul's Korean Way of Zen*. Honolulu, HI: University of Hawaii Press, 1991.

Chödrön, Pema. *Living Beautifully: With Uncertainty and Change*. Boston: Shambhala Publications, 2012.

Epstein, Mark. *Thoughts Without a Thinker.* New York: Basic Books, 1995.

Ford, James Ishmael. *In This Very Moment: A Simple Guide to Zen Buddhism*. Boston: Skinner House Books, 2002.

———. *Zen Master Who?: A Guide to the People and Stories of Zen*. Somerville, MA: Wisdom Publications, 2006.

———. *If You're Lucky Your Heart Will Break: Field Notes from a Zen Life*. Somerville, MA: Wisdom Publications, 2012.

Glassman, Bernie. *Bearing Witness: A Zen Master's Lessons in Making Peace*. New York: Bell Tower, 1998.

Goldstein, Joseph. *One Dharma: The Emerging Western Buddhism*. New York: HarperCollins, 2002.

Goldstein, Joseph and Jack Kornfield. *Seeking the Heart of Wisdom: The Path of Insight Meditation*. Boston: Shambhala Publications, 1987.

Gunaratana, Bhante Henepola. *Mindfulness in Plain English*. Somerville, MA: Wisdom Publications, 1996.

Hanh, Thich Nhat. *The Miracle of Mindfulness: An Introduction to the Practice of Meditation*. Boston: Beacon Press, 1975.

————.*The Heart of the Buddha's Teachings: Transforming Suffering into Peace, Joy, and Liberation*. New York: Broadway Books, 1998.

Kabat-Zinn, Jon. *Wherever You Go, There You Are: Mindfulness Meditation in Everyday Life*. New York: Hyperion, 1994.

————. *Coming to Our Senses: Healing Ourselves and the World Through Mindfulness*. New York: Hyperion, 2005.

Krishnamurti, Jiddu. *This Light in Oneself: True Meditation*. Boston: Shambhala Publications, 1999.

Kornfield, Jack. *A Path With Heart: A Guide Through the Perils and Promises of Spiritual Life*. New York: Bantam Book, 1993.

Levine, Stephen. *A Gradual Awakening*. New York: Anchor Books, 1979.

Loori, John Daido. *The Eight Gates of Zen: A Program of Zen Training*. Boston: Shambhala Publications, 1994.

————. *The Zen of Creativity: Cultivating Your Artistic Life*. New York: Ballentine Books, 2004.

Rahula, Walpola. *What the Buddha Taught*. New York: Grove Press, 1959.

Rinpoche, Yongey Mingyur. *The Joy of Living: Unlocking the Secret and Science of Happiness*. New York: Harmony Books, 2007.

Rosenberg, Larry. *Breath by Breath: The Liberating Practice of Insight Meditation.* Boston: Shambhala Publications, 1998.

————. *Living in the Light of Death: On the Art of Being Truly Alive.* Boston: Shambhala Publications, 2000.

Rynick, David. *This Truth Never Fails: A Zen Memoir in Four Seasons.* Somerville, MA: Wisdom Publications, 2012.

Salzberg, Sharon. *Lovingkindness: The Revolutionary Art of Happiness.* Boston: Shambhala Publications, 1995.

————. *Faith: Trusting Your Deepest Experience.* New York: Riverhead Books, 2002.

Santorelli, Saki. *Heal Thy Self: Lessons on Mindfulness in Medicine.* New York: Bell Tower, 1999.

Sheng-yen, Chang. *Hoofprints of the Ox: Principles of the Chan Buddhist Path.* New York: Oxford University Press, 2001.

Sumedho, Ajahn. *The Mind and the Way: Buddhist Reflections on Life.* Somerville, MA: Wisdom Publications, 1995.

Suzuki, Shunryu. *Zen Mind, Beginner's Mind.* Boston: Shambhala Publications, 2011.

Thera Nyanaponika. *The Heart of Buddhist Meditation.* York Beach, ME: Samuel Weiser, Inc, 1965.

Wallace, B. Alan. *Tibetan Buddhism from the Ground Up: A Practical Approach for Modern Life.* Somerville, MA: Wisdom Publications, 1993.

# GLOSSARY

This glossary covers the words in Sanskrit, Pali, Chinese, and Japanese used in this book and in common usage among Western Buddhists. It is by no means an exhaustive glossary of Buddhist terminology.

The editors thank James Ishmael Ford for permis sion to use certain glossary definitions found in Ford's book *Zen Master Who?*, published in 2006 by Wisdom Publications.

**Amitabha Buddha.** Sanskrit word meaning literally "Boundless Light" or "Immeasurable Life." The primary object of devotion within Pure Land Buddhism. In Japanese, *Amida*.

**Arhat.** A Sanskrit word literally meaning "a Holy One." A self-realized person no longer bound by the cycles of rebirth.

**Attachments.** A metaphorical English term often used to explain the mental and emotional clinging to self that is the cause of suffering described in the second noble truth. See *four noble truths.*

**Authorized.** Buddhist schools have different standards for how a person is recognized and empowered as teacher. Without any central hierarchy of authority, and with teaching authority largely given individually by a teacher to a student, variation among the different schools and teaching lineages can be considerable. Some schools place great importance on formal authorization and encourage Buddhist students to take it very seriously in considering any relationship with someone who identifies as a teacher. In other schools, authorization receives less emphasis.

**Avalokitesvara.** The Sanskrit name for the archetype of compassion. In Japanese, *Kannon* or *Kanzeon*; in Chinese, *Kwan-Yin* or *Guanyin*; in Korean, *Kwan Um.*

**Awakening.** An English word used in the translation of the original teaching of the Buddha, his first words after meditating under the Bodhi tree and seeing the morning star and attaining enlightenment: "I see in this moment all the beings of the world and I awake together." The metaphor of awakening from sleep has been used to describe the insight and understanding of our true nature and living within that insight and understanding. See *enlightenment.*

**Bardo.** A Tibetan word meaning "intermediate state," usually describing a state between lives on earth.

**Bodhisattva.** A Sanskrit word that describes the ideal of the Mahayana School of Buddhism, i.e., to become a person who is fully awake and is committed to awakening others. In Mandarin, *pusa.*

**Bodhi tree.** An ancient sacred fig tree with heart-shaped leaves located in Bodhgaya, in the northeastern corner of present day India. The Buddha became fully enlightened while sitting in meditation under this tree.

**Buddha.** Sanskrit for "one who is awakened." The word is used for the historic Buddha, Siddhartha Gautama, but may also be applied to mythic earlier Buddhas, Buddhas to come, or our own essential nature.

**Buddhadharma.** The truth and teachings of the Buddha; another way to say Buddhism.

**Buddha nature.** The essential nature of all sentient beings understood in a non-dualistic way.

**Buddha way.** The path that one must follow to see one's true nature and to become a Buddha.

**Ch'an Buddhism.** The Zen school in its original Chinese use. The word is derived from the Chinese *channa,* and the Sanskrit *dhyana,* meaning "concentration" or "meditation." This school of Buddhism emphasizes meditation disciplines, influenced by Chinese Taoism, and is the root of the Zen schools imported to the West.

**Chant.** To speak aloud sutras or poems in liturgical services.

**Dalai Lama.** The highest ranking lama (teacher) in Tibetan Buddhism, who serves as the head of the theocracy that existed in Tibet before the Chinese invasion. The Dalai Lama is not recognized as the head of all the schools of Tibetan Buddhism but is regarded as an incarnation of Avalokitesvara, and carries a mythological role as the savior of the Tibetan people. The fame of the fourteenth and current Dalai Lama has resulted in many Westerners looking at him as the Buddhist "pope," a misunderstanding of his role.

**Dharma.** A Sanskrit word meaning "law." In English, when used without capitalization it usually means a "constituent element of reality." With a capital "D" it usually means the Buddhist teachings or the Buddha way as a whole.

**Dharma door or dharma gate.** An element of the Buddhist teachings or an element of everyday reality that provides an opportunity for awakening.

**Dharma name.** A new name given to a Zen student by the teacher at the time the student receives the Buddhist precepts and formally identifies as a Buddhist.

**Dharma talk.** A talk given by an authorized teacher to a *sangha,* or community of students.

**Dharma wheel.** The wheel of the dharma or life, an ancient circular symbol of the Buddhist path to enlightenment that has eight spokes. In Sanskrit, *dharmacakra*; in Pali, *dhammacakka*; in Mandarin, *falun*.

**Dukkha.** A Sanskrit word meaning "suffering, anguish, dis-ease." The unsettled sense of the human condition described in the first of the four noble truths. See *four noble truths*.

**Eight-fold path**. Buddhist teachings around meditation, morality, and wisdom applied to the everyday life. These were in Buddha's first sermon as the fourth noble truth. The eight components are right (or correct) view, resolve, speech, action, livelihood, effort, mindfulness, and concentration. See *four noble truths*.

**Enlightenment.** The insight and understanding of our true nature, and living within that insight and understanding. See *awakening*.

**Enso.** A Japanese word for circle. A subject of Japanese Zen calligraphy symbolizing both absolute enlightenment and the universe as whole.

**Four noble truths.** In his first sermon, Buddha proclaimed a way for human beings to heal themselves and the world. These truths are the most concise summary of the Buddha Way to this day. The four noble truths are: First, life is impermanent and has suffering. Second, this suffering arises as a result of our desires and attachments. Third, freedom from this suffering is possible. Fourth, the path that leads to this freedom is an eight-fold path (See *eight-fold path*)."

**Gatha.** A metered and often rhythmic verse of poetry or a phrase in the historic Indian languages of Prakrit and Sanskrit. The word comes from the Sanskrit/Prakrit root *gai,* meaning to speak, sing, recite, or extol. So *gatha* can mean speech, verse, or a song.

**Great vows.** The vow of a bodhisattva to work for the liberation of all beings, often chanted at the end of Zen liturgies.

**Inka shomei.** The ceremony that formally recognizes a new Zen master's deepest realization and authority to teach.

**Jukai.** A Japanese term for receiving the precepts, the moral and ethical teachings of Buddhism. The ceremony has some parallels to Christian confirmation, in which an individual proclaims his or her intention to live according to the Buddhist precepts.

**Kalachakra.** A Sanskrit word referring to both a deity within Vajrayana (Tibetan) Buddhism and to the philosophies and meditation practices contained within the scripture *Kalachakra Tantra* and its many commentaries.

**Karma.** A philosophical doctrine of both Hinduism and Buddhism. In Buddhism, karma arises from the doctrine of "dependent origination," i.e., that everything in the universe arises out of causes and conditions. In the West, karma is widely misunderstood in popular culture as a cosmic moral law. The simplest way to understand karma is that everything has causes and consequences that help us understand why and how it exists.

**Koan.** Japanese word meaning "a public case," as in a legal document. In Zen, a theme or point to be clarified. Usually expressed in the form of a story or a question, a koan is an expression of the unity of relative and absolute.

**Kowtow.** An English interpretation of the words *kòu tóu* in Mandarin Chinese, referring to the act of deep respect shown by kneeling and bowing so low as to have one's head touching the ground. In the West, the word usually is used with derogation. In Japanese Zen, bowing in respect in usually referred to as *prostration*.

**Kwan-Yin.** See *Avalokitesvara* (also seen as Kwan Shih Yin, with *Shih* as an honorific term).

**Lama.** The title for a Tibetan teacher of the Buddha dharma.

**Lay ordination.** In some Zen traditions, *jukai* is referred to as lay ordination. The formal ceremony involves explicitly assuming a relationship with a teacher and teaching lineage, and receiving a *rakusu*. See *jukai* and *rakusu*.

**Lineage.** The chain of authorization among Buddhist teachers. In some Zen traditions, a lineage chart is given to a student receiving *jukai* that traces the lineage of the teacher back to Buddha. It is widely acknowledged that the most ancient parts of the lineage include legend and mythology and cannot be proven. However, the lineage chain from eighth-century China is well documented and accepted and very important, since it is not about "diploma" recognition but recognition of realization from a teacher to student: "mind to mind transmission." See *jukai*.

**Lotus.** A plant and flower common in Asia widely used as a Buddhist symbol and usually depicted with eight petals representing the eight-fold path.

*Lotus Sutra.* One of the most popular and influential Mayahana Buddhist texts, said to be based on a sermon Buddha gave toward the end of his life. The text focuses on teaching skilful means of living through parables, and is especially important to Japanese Nichiren Buddhist sects.

**Loving-kindness.** An English translation of the Buddhist term *metta;* a meditation practice within Theravadin Buddhist traditions that has become widely encouraged by Western teachers who trained with Theravadin teachers. In the Tibetan schools the metta practice is associated with tonglen practice, and invites breathing in the suffering of others and breathing out love and compassion.

**Lunar new year.** In Asian countries where Buddhism originated, the new year is celebrated according to a lunar calendar. Asian Buddhists celebrate the holiday both within and beyond their temples.

**Mahasthamaprapta.** One of the eight great bodhisattvas in Mahayana Buddhism that represents the power of wisdom; often depicted in a trinity with Amitabha and Avalokitesvara (Guanyin), especially in Pure Land Buddhism. The name literally means "arrival of the great strength." See *bodhisattva*.

**Mahayana.** A Sanskrit word meaning "the Great Vehicle" or "Great Way." One of the two principal streams of Buddhism (see also *Theravada*) that champions the idea of the bodhisattva. Zen is a school within Mahayana Buddhism. See *bodhisattva*.

**Meditation.** The practice of concentration and expansive awareness that is encouraged by many Buddhist traditions as a path to enlightenment.

**Merit.** Buddhist and Hindu concept meaning that which accumulates as a result of good deeds, acts, or thoughts and which carries over to later life or the next life. Such merit contributes to a person's growth toward liberation.

**Metta.** Sanskrit word meaning compassion, good will, loving-kindness. Together with *vipassana* and *shamatha*, one of the three meditative practices taught in early Buddhism.

**Mindfulness.** A quality of attention to either internal mental and physical processes of meditation or to the outside world, with the intention of experiencing the unity of the two.

**Monk.** A man ordained within the *Vinaya* tradition who has made a commitment to a monastic life. Most Buddhist traditions use the word to describe male monastics, but some American traditions use the word *monastic* as a gender-neutral term.

**Mudra.** A symbolic or ritual hand gesture in Hinduism and Buddhism.

**Nirvana.** A Sanskrit word meaning "blown out" (as in a candle); in Pali, *nibbana.* In Hindu philosophy, it means union with the Brahman (Supreme Being). In the Buddhist context, it refers to "the imperturbable stillness of mind after the fires of desire, aversion, and delusion have been finally extinguished" (quotation from Richard Gombrich, *Theravada Buddhism: A Social History from Ancient Benares to Modern Colombo*).

**Nun.** A woman ordained within the *Vinaya* tradition who has made a commitment to a monastic life. Most Buddhist traditions use the word to describe female monastics, but some American traditions use the word *monastic* as a gender-neutral term.

**Phowa.** A Vajrayana (Tibetan) Buddhist meditation practice directed at conscious dying and the transfer of consciousness after death.

**Practice.** The daily spiritual disciplines of Buddhism.

**Precepts.** The moral and ethical teachings of Buddhism. There are several versions of them, including the 250 Vinaya vows for monastics, the 16 bodhisattva vows, and the 5 traditional precepts of lay Buddhism. These five precepts include the vows to refrain from killing, lying, stealing, misusing sexuality, and intoxication.

**Pure Land Buddhism.** One of the principal schools of Mahayana Buddhism, called *Jingtuzong* in Chinese and *Jodo* or *Jodo Shinshu* in Japanese. As a faith-oriented school, Pure Land focuses on devotion to Amitabha Buddha, and out of that devotion rebirth in the Pure Land, where liberation is easier to obtain. See *Amitabha Buddha*.

**Pusa.** See *bodhisattva*.

**Rakusu.** A bib-like vestment worn by both lay practitioners who have received the precepts and priests in Japanese and Korean forms of Buddhism, including the Zen schools. It represents the robe of the Buddha in traditional Buddhism.

**Realize.** Used frequently in descriptions of the process of awakening, as in "to realize your Buddha nature."

**Reincarnation.** A Hindu belief that life is continuous through multiple births and deaths. It has carried over into the theologies of some, but not all, Buddhist schools.

**Samadhi.** From the Sanskrit word meaning concentration or absorption. The term describes the form of meditation taught in Buddhism, particularly the Zen school.

**Sangha.** A Pali and Sanskrit word meaning assembly, association, or community. In Asian Buddhism the word refers to the monastic community of ordained monks and nuns. In Western Buddhism the word is used more frequently to refer to a community of Buddhist practitioners, both lay and ordained.

**Sati.** A Pali word used in Buddhism to mean awareness or skillful attentiveness.

**Sesshin.** A Japanese word meaning literally "to touch the mind-heart," used to describe an intensive meditation retreat, most commonly lasting from three to seven days.

**Shambhala.** In Tibetan tradition, the name of a mythical kingdom, which became associated with the Pure Land. It is referred to in the Kalachakra Tantra texts. In Western Buddhism, Shambhala is the name of a network of meditation centers in the lineage of Chogyam Trungpa Rinpoche, one of the early Tibetan teachers to take up residence and teach in the United States.

**Shikantaza.** A Japanese word meaning "just sitting"; the meditative practice of pure presence that is commonly associated with the Soto school, but is in fact the basis of all Zen discipline.

**Soto.** The Japanese Zen school, most closely associated with the practice of shikantaza.

**Sutra.** A Sanskrit word meaning thread, used to describe spiritual texts.

**Ta Shih Chi.** One of the two principal bodhisattvas of Pure Land Buddhism. See *bodhisattva*.

**Tai chi.** An internal Chinese martial art practiced both for defense purposes and for its health benefits.

**Tanhā.** A Pali word for thirst, commonly understood as craving or desire. In the second of the four noble truths, the Buddha pointed to tanhā as the cause of suffering. See *four noble truths*.

**Tantra.** A Sanskrit word with many meanings, notably "loom," applied to a Hindu spiritual practice, teaching, and theology. In Buddhism, tantra is a body of teachings and practices within Vajrayana Buddhism, one of the three major schools and the school associated with Tibet.

**Teacher.** An English word used as a title of respect. Many Western Buddhist communities use the formal titles for teachers in the Sanskrit, Chinese, or Japanese languages.

**Teisho.** A talk given by a Zen master during a meditation retreat or *sesshin*. See *sesshin*.

**Temple.** A Buddhist religious center for devotional and meditative practice.

**Theravada.** A Pali word for "Way of the Elders." One of the two principal schools of Buddhism, associated with the *arhat* ideal, i.e., that self-realization means that one is no longer bound by the cycles of rebirth.

**Three marks of existence.** Greed, anger, and ignorance. Also known as the "three poisons." These are the conditions which create suffering.

**Three poisons.** Greed, anger, and ignorance. Also known as the "three marks of existence."

**Three pure precepts.** The most concise summary of the Buddhist moral code: avoid evil, create good, and actualize good for others.

**Three treasures.** The Buddha, the dharma, and the sangha. Each of these has a historical or literal referent and a more mystical referent. For example, Buddha is both the historical figure and the reality of Buddha nature embodied in the lineage of Buddhas throughout space and time. Buddhists "take refuge" in these realities to sustain their practice. Also known as the "three refuges." See *dharma* and *sangha*.

**Tonglen.** A Tibetan word for "giving and taking" and the name of a Tibetan Buddhist meditation practice that involves taking on the suffering of others with the in-breath and, on the out-breath, giving happiness and success to all sentient beings.

**Upaya.** The expedient or skillful means used to guide a student toward enlightenment.

**Vajrasattva.** A bodhisattva in the Mahayana and Vajrayana traditions. See *bodhisattva*.

**Vajrayana.** A complex and multi-faceted system of Buddhist thought, evolved over centuries. The third major Buddhist school, evolving beyond the Mahayana tradition as a "third turning of the wheel" or evolutionary stage in Buddhist thought and practice. Vajrayana practice settled in Tibet after the eighth century and has been vigorously taught in America by exiled Tibetan teachers and their students.

**Vesak.** A holiday celebrating Buddha observed by South Asian Buddhists variously in the fifth or sixth lunar month.

**Vihara.** Sanskrit and Pali word for a Buddhist monastery. In Thailand and China the term means a shrine hall.

**Vinaya.** The Sanskrit name for the code of morality and traditional precepts for monastic ordination in Buddhism.

**Vipassana.** A Sanskrit word meaning "insight." Together with *metta* and *shamatha*, one of the three meditation practices taught in early Buddhism. The name is commonly given to a school of Buddhism brought to America from South Asia and taught as "insight meditation."

**Vows.** Promises or commitments made by Buddhist practitioners.

**Walking meditation.** Also known in Zen practice as *kinhin*. The meditator maintains the meditative practice while rising from the cushion and walking for several minutes at a slower, then faster, pace.

**Way.** An English translation of a word used in Chinese Taoism for the spiritual path, and adopted by Buddhism. In liturgical chants the phrase "Buddha Way" often appears.

**Zafu.** A cushion used for sitting meditation, often placed on top of a flat cushion known as a *zebuton*.

**Zazen.** A Japanese word meaning "sitting Zen," the formal practice of Zen meditation.

**Zen master.** A teacher in a Zen Buddhist tradition who has received formal authorization (or transmission) to teach.

# Acknowledgments

Wayne Arnason would like to thank his teachers, John Daido Loori, Roshi; Geoffrey Shugen Arnold, Sensei; and Konrad Ryushin Marchaj, Sensei, of the Mountains and Rivers Order; and James Ishmael Ford of the Boundless Way Zen Community, for their wisdom and patience. The River Rocks Sangha and the members of West Shore Unitarian Universalist Church are a constant blessing. This project would not have been realized without the inspiration and loving partnership of Rev. Kathleen Rolenz.

Sam Trumbore would like to thank the teachers at the Insight Meditation Society, whose adaptation of Theravadan Buddhism for Westerners forms the foundation of my meditation practice. I am deeply grateful for the Forest Refuge retreat center in Barre, Massachusetts, where I go to do practice. I am also grateful to James Ishmael Ford who coaxed me into the UUBF at the UUA General Assembly in Phoenix in 1997. My thanks to both my congregation, the First Unitarian Univeralist Society of Albany, New York, and my wife, Philomena Moriarty, for their patience and support while Wayne and I were assembling and editing this book.

Both Wayne Arnason and Sam Trumbore would like to thank Erik Walker Wikstrom for his provocation to imagine this book during his term of service on the Skinner House Editorial Board. We are deeply grateful to our editors, Mary Benard and Marshall Hawkins, for their care, persistence, and encouragement. Our contributing authors have been a delight to work with, displaying non-attachment in great measure throughout the editing process!